Singing for Supper

A busker's tale

By
A W Lindahl

MAPLE
PUBLISHERS

Singing for supper

Author: A W Lindahl

Copyright © 2023 A W Lindahl

The right of A W Lindahl to be identified as author of this work has been asserted by the author in accordance with section 77 and 78 of the Copyright, Designs and Patents Act 1988.

First Published in 2023

ISBN 978-1-83538-013-0 (Paperback)
    978-1-83538-014-7 (E-Book)

Book cover and Book layout by:
    White Magic Studios
    www.whitemagicstudios.co.uk

Published by:
    Maple Publishers
    Fairbourne Drive, Atterbury,
    Milton Keynes,
    MK10 9RG, UK
    www.maplepublishers.com

Contents

The creature in me

I am a wolf in search of the river where the water flows in from the stream,

tangled roots in the sycamore trees and the leaves turn gold from green.

I'll run the path of the river till it joins the sea. Jump the waves of the ocean like the creature in me, the creature in me, the creature in me.

I am a seagull far from the shore in a town where the river runs through.

I forage food and I drink dirty water, I'm a shadow of the bird I once knew.

I'll fly the length of the river till it joins the sea, skim the waves of the ocean like the creature in me, the creature in me, the creature in me.

I am human in search of my freedom on a river that's calm and serene,

I'll float away to a place I can stay on a raft made of sycamore tree.

Drift the length of the river till it joins the sea.

Surf the waves of the ocean like the creature in me the creature in me, the creature in me.

To my lovely boys. My birth sons, Oliver, Charlie and Adam and my foster sons, Pav, Dan, Lewis and Joseph.

Also, to my husband, James Bristow, and my brothers, Patrick and Daniel. My sister-in-law, Les. My childhood friend, Vicky. My Dad and his family, my step siblings. My Swedish family, Barbro, Anna, Linnea, Bjorn.

To my band, Garry, Mark, Ralph and Rob. Also, to my music followers and all of my good friends, you know who you are. Also, to my mentors and those who have encouraged me, believed in me and helped me decide on titles etc. Ray who made my leather music accessories, whom I exchange stories and have coffee with, every Wednesday. To Jane Kelly who started Hennesea with me originally as a duo and believed in my songs, who helped produce the first album 'Lost for words' with her amazing vocals and expertise and pushed me to get back into music.

From beyond the grave, Mum, my inspiration and Mormor and Morfar who never gave up on me.

Finally, a special thanks to my travelling companion and friend, Jane, who shared many experiences with me.

This book wouldn't exist without you.

Chapter 1

In September 2022 I returned from a trip of a lifetime. Although it was short, I came home with a new vision of what I wanted my future to look like. New hopes and dreams and a big picture, full of possibilities. The people I met, the bands I went to see and the books I read, all gave me a new focus. I wanted to stay on that high, learn from that experience and use the time I now have on my hands to do something constructive, creative and unique.

My children have grown up, we have moved house, down sized and I am working part time, singing in care homes. It's more of a vocation than a job and it's teaching me a lot about dementia and opening up my eyes to what could possibly be right around the corner but more importantly to the incredible effect that music has on people, the way it can spark memories, awaken the brain as well as calm and relax the mind from stress and anxiety.

My philosophy in life has always been 'play it by ear' see what happens. Plans can fail to materialise but non plans are when things just happen unexpectedly and better still, with no expectations. I hadn't planned my trip; it was a surprise from the people that mean the most to me in life. My vision involves music, travel and books, as well as all the stories that I collect along the way. I continue to 'play it by ear' when it comes to my social life which drives my friends nuts, but I now have a loose but very self-indulgent plan. I do believe in setting yourself goals and I think that anything can be achieved within reason so taking the right path is important, as well as staying focused. A plan is all about structure and formality, following a path that is suggested because others have found success that way. The less travelled road is where the creative energy flows. Going to Nashville last year was a dream of mine since I was a child and last year the timing was perfect. I guess what I'm saying is I want to keep being spontaneous and jumping at chance adventures but at the same time stick to my goals. Goal number one. Write a book.

This book is to my boys: Adam, Charlie, Ollie, Lewis, Joseph, Pav, and Dan. I am so proud of them all, they have grown into the most wonderful men. They see me and respect me for being me and I am so blessed to call them family. Sometimes I tell them snippets about how my life was before having children but I'm hoping if they read this book, they will know me a bit more. Maybe even know themselves a bit better. All I want is for them to follow their own dreams and be happy and whole.

My boys, from the left, Adam, Pav, Dan, Lewis, Oliver, Joseph, Charlie.

Life is a journey, full of obstacles, difficulties, falling over, getting back up, making mistakes, fixing mistakes, repeating mistakes, and learning from them. I'm still learning, expanding my mind, and building my confidence.

I've been writing songs since I was about 11, when I discovered chords. Although my lyrics were quite simple and basic with a lot of naivety, the feeling of creating something from nothing became addictive and a source of therapy to alleviate frustration, anger and sadness. Not only was it my 'go to' and escape, but it was also my distraction and still is, although now I am making it a priority.

I like to use metaphors when I write songs, although it takes a lot more thought as to what is coming out of my mind and whether it makes sense. It usually does, and I must trust in that even though some people don't understand and wonder what the song is about. I like that though because I can hide behind a code that only some curious types of people will try to unravel.

'The Journey' feels like a suitable song to start my book with. There will be more throughout, which might link in some way to the chapter that follows. It's difficult to explain the meaning behind certain songs but to me those are the best ones. They come from a place deep within, like a dream, they don't need much thought, just a channel from the subconscious mind to pen, paper, instrument, voice. It doesn't happen often and there is no plan. I can only say that something comes along that triggers it, the rest is already there just waiting to be released. The entire process leaves me feeling warm and fuzzy. A weight I didn't know I was carrying is lifted, a secret unfolded, a feeling revealed, or a memory released. Even fictional songs have an element of truth about them because to find a character to sing about one must have known or at least met a similar person and studied or observed them. You may be writing about a time or an event you have experienced but forgotten about.

'The Warrior' and 'Mandolin man' are both fictional characters based loosely on people I have met. I'll introduce the songs to you later but first I'm going to take you on a journey.

The Journey

I machete through the trees to find the meaning,
behind the place in which I had been dreaming,
If I walk along this road, would I fall on jagged stones?
Would I break my bones and keep on tumbling?
Now I'm cutting through the forest of my mind,
wading in the river of my dreams, taking giant steps across the ditches of my thoughts,
Running through the wasteland as I try to stop myself from going under.
It's a long dangerous journey to be walking,
And I am doing lots of thinking to myself,
It's a long way down to be falling,
If I fell, I'd only hurt myself.
Now I'm ploughing through the jungle,
Moving onwards, ignoring all the signs and heading forwards,
Trying to find the gap between the mountains in my head,
Trying to find that certain place, trying to find that place I'm dreaming of.
Now I've fallen blind and dizzy in the sand,
There's nothing here at all just desert land,
I'm lying all alone I'll never find my way back home,
The bridges are all broken, the paths are overgrown.
The ditches have got wider, my world is falling in,
The ditches have got wide, and my world is falling in.

Song writing to me is like writing poems or short stories and putting a tune to them. For me, to love a song it must mean something. I need to feel it and be inspired by it. I don't expect everyone to understand my lyrics but if they resonate with at least one person then I have succeeded. If the song writing process has taken my mind away from a difficult situation that I'm facing, then it has been my medicine and given me strength to get through tough stuff and carry on; my creative band aid!

If this, so far strikes a 'chord' with you then please continue to read....

Intro:

I have a band called Hennesea. We play regularly in and around Malvern. If you see us playing in one of the many old pubs or music venues, call in and say 'hi'. Alternatively, you can look us up online - www.Hennesea.com

The band. From left Garry, Mark, me, Ralph and Rob.

My band members are my music family - Garry, Mark, Ralph and Rob, the ingredients that all together produce the Hennesea sound. Interestingly we are all so different. We couldn't really be more dissimilar in personality, our family and

professional lives, but we share that one passion - music, and it works. Musically our backgrounds are also quite different, so we each bring our individual styles into the band. I introduce the songs in my way and by the time we've learned them well enough to perform they may have an edge of rock, blues, reggae, or country with a twist of world music, of Greek, French or Swedish influence. Quite an eclectic mishmash which is why I struggle to decide our genre.

I am married to James Bristow, a childhood friend of mine, and we have 3 sons. I became a foster carer in my late 20's so I have raised and cared for dozens of children in the last 25 years, some of whom I am still close to and are very much part of my family. I have recently retired from fostering and although I have my band and my part time job, I finally have the time to reflect on my past and write about the parts of my life that I feel have contributed to the person I am today.

Looking back on events that have happened in my life is helping me to answer the questions that people sometimes ask. We are conditioned and expected to explain everything. Questions I am often asked besides "What's the song about?" are "What is your genre?" and "Who were you inspired by?" I'm still trying to work these things out. By the end of this book, we might have found the answers to some of these questions. I love all types of music, I don't have favourites, but I like to listen to songs that encourage me, tempt me into learning or stir up emotions. I am inspired by many singers and bands, buskers, and poets too. I tell a story and when I can put it with a tune it becomes something I can sing. I refrain from calling myself a musician, a poet, or a singer. I play the guitar and harmonica, but I could never master either of them, they are just my writing tools. When someone can relate and feel emotion from hearing one of my songs, I feel great but on the flip side I can beat myself up with irrational feelings of self-doubt. Being the creative type goes hand in hand with being overly sensitive. I see a compliment as kindness. I don't like my voice and performing is a huge risk that can go terribly wrong. So why do I do it?

Spider in a jar

Why do I shake when I'm angry? Why do I shiver when I'm scared? Why can't I smile when I hear good news? My emotions are driving me mad.

How do I make sense of my feelings? How do I know what to feel? How do I know whether to laugh or cry when I don't even know what is real?

I'm like a spider in a jar, trying to find a way out to get back into the world where people hear me scream and shout. I'm like a horse in transit heading for a fall. I look my best, smile with the rest as there's nowhere else to go.

How does one define sanity? How do I know if it's sane to scream and shout, laugh, and sing naked in the rain?Like a child on a roundabout, neither feeling pleasure or pain, but a sense of helplessness and desire to do it all over again.

I pour down my last drop of wine and let the bottle crash to the ground and I imagine I'm on that roundabout and fall asleep without a sound.

I'm like a spider in a jar trying to find a way out to get back into the world where people hear me scream and shout. I'm like a horse in transit heading for a fall. I look my best, smile with the rest as there's nowhere else to go.

Song writing can be a way of turning a negative into a positive. Like many things in life, we tend to only see the bad and criticise ourselves and others. Some of people's most endearing qualities are the things that they least like about themselves. Some of the most dreaded events can turn out to be the best ones and a bad day can turn into a most productive day. If you take advantage of your emotions, you can create some of your best work.

Some years ago, having finally completed a level 4 in sports massage therapy I was giving in my paper to be marked before the deadline. The college was in Kidderminster, an hour's drive away from Malvern. I'd worked hard to finish it on time and was ready to hand it in. When I arrived at the college I parked up and ran in to meet my tutor. However, she had forgotten we had an appointment and I spent an hour waiting and running around looking for her. I was getting myself into a manic state and when I finally gave up and went out to my car, to my absolute fury there was a £60 parking fine stuck on the windscreen. We've all had days like that, and they are never usually as bad as we make out them to be at the time, but the combination of stresses builds up and triggers something; it's like a button within us is suddenly pressed which opens a box of emotions and everything comes flooding out all at once. My rage in the Kidderminster carpark as I fumbled with my car keys in the rain brought on a deluge of tears. As I was driving home, I got stuck behind a horse box, going 30 mph on a dual carriageway and the words came to me of a new song. They were not the sort of lyrics that I would remember so I pulled into a petrol station and bought a pen. I had a scrap of paper in my bag, so I scribbled down the words in the car before driving back home. The basic tune was already there in my head, so I grabbed my guitar and within a couple of hours I had a new song.

My advice to any passionate song writer though is to sing your own songs and don't be afraid of your voice. You are a storyteller, and no one can tell your story like you can. Easier said than done? Well, if I can do it anyone can. On my first album 'Lost for words' Jane Kelly did most of the lead vocals. She has an amazingly strong, trained voice. It seemed absurd for me to sing lead, so I stuck to backing vocals. I love that album and her voice did the songs justice but in hindsight it was an excuse on my behalf and when Jane unexpectedly left the band, I was stuck with a bunch of songs that I had to learn to sing and project myself amongst a band of loud musicians. With a bit of work and thought we turned the songs back to their roots and brought them to life again in a much more laid-back way.

Song writing can certainly be learned by anyone but achieving something that you, as a writer, will enjoy listening to is something else. We are our biggest critics. I have written so many songs that I've lost count. They don't all work but every one of them is a useful lesson, I see it as training. If I feel the need to pick it apart until the original idea no longer exists, then I know that it is not to be. Something that I struggle with is when someone wants to collaborate. They say, 'Let's write something.' I've never been to see a counsellor or psychotherapist before, but I can imagine my mind closing so tightly. Words come to me through solitude, sometimes when I'm extremely tired or when I'm out running. I can never plan to sit and write a song. I love my own company and I am extremely fortunate to have the time and space to write this book.

In my mind I am about to step back in time to when the world was quite different. In some ways it feels like we have gone around in circles but in others we have moved on in leaps and bounds. In one word I would say the biggest change of all is communication. Technically, in theory things are easier as we now have computers and mobile phones, we are all connected through the internet, everything is quicker. Personally, I think we are losing our ability to interact like we used to and our general survival instincts are becoming disempowered. Because of communication and the development of technology music has changed, the way it's recorded, and programmed using computers, the playing of instruments is no longer absolutely needed or even being able to sing in tune. It's debatable as to whether quality is better or worse now and I wouldn't like to get into that one but on a personal level I feel we have lost something special, that rawness and emotion that is felt through a musical instrument and a vocal with minimal effects on it. I'll leave it there.

My name is Anna, daughter of Eva and Andrew Watts, my mother was Swedish. She died when she was 42 leaving Daniel age, 10, Patrick and myself who were not so young but only just out there braving the world. It was a traumatic time in my life. Mum was my rock, she was the mortar that kept our family together, she was strong but gentle, fun and loving.

Eva came to England as an au pair when she was 18. Her dream was to go to Australia, but her parents objected as it was too far away. They wanted her to stay in Sweden and finish her education but the rebel she was, she defied her parents and as a compromise she decided on England instead. She travelled alone but had a family to go to when she arrived. Whilst in the UK as well as working she trained to become a nurse. She met Andrew, he was the brother of the lady of the house where she was working, the youngest son of Canon Wilfred and Kitty Watts. He too had defied his parents who had put him through expensive private schools and gone his own way working for the local tree surgeon. He was handsome and rugged, with blond wavy hair, and Eva fell in love with him the moment she met him.

He was visiting his sister. I think he'd been advised to check out the new au pair and wasn't disappointed. They embarked on a relationship and much to her parents' disapproval she got pregnant. Later the two of them went to Sweden where they were soon to be wed. They returned to England, husband and wife, and lived for a short time at Hambleden rectory where Andrew had grown up. By the time the baby was 2 they had their own place and shortly after, I was born.

My Grandmother and her husband, Canon Watts, had separated, and she had bought two kiln cottages in Binfield heath, one for herself and one for my parents which she sold to them for an affordable price. The cottages, very run down and in need of renovation were nestled within neglected woodland of about 4 acres. My father who then had his own business as a tree surgeon cleared a lot of the trees and filled in the swamps over the years. Our cottage was eventually extended into a large 4-bedroom house.

Growing up in the remote area of Binfield heath was a privilege and we were the envy of our friends, being out in the sticks but it was lonely at times. I learned to entertain myself and enjoy my own company. I developed a good imagination at an early age which still serves me today. It can be a blessing and a curse as I'm always looking for my next big adventure and I can sometimes feel stifled by people and their expectations of me as well as their demands. Like my mother, I am a free spirit, desperate for wings so I can fly.

Mum played guitar, self-taught at an early age. She had a book of songs all handwritten neatly herself with chords carefully worked out by listening to records from the 60's -70's. Like many others of her generation, she was passionately into the Beatles, Elvis Presley and Abba but she also loved the less mainstream artists of that era like Gordon Lightfoot, Joan Baez and Ralph McTell.

I was in awe of my mother; she was quite beautiful with long auburn hair. She wore flowing dresses, knee-high boots and lots of jewellery. I remember staring into her emerald, green eyes which had tiny specks of brown around the iris, and imagining that they were little hens pecking in the grass.

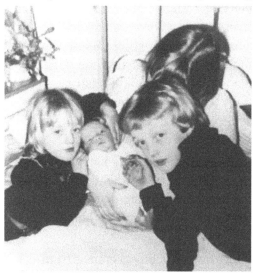

Me on the left, Patrick, baby Daniel and Mum.

By the time I was 9 years old my younger brother, Daniel, came into the world. I felt I knew him before he was born as I would sit beside mum every evening, feeling the growing baby. When I first set eyes on him, I adored him. I grew up quickly as I was no longer the youngest and I was given little jobs to do. I loved being included in the raising of Daniel and for him I'm sure it was like having two mums. I started dressing like my mum, borrowing her clothes and jewellery, experimenting with green eye shadows and mascara but playing her records became a passion. She had such an assortment, and I played every one of them. I loved vinyl, I would carefully play them on her gramophone whilst reading the sleeves inside and out, I was fascinated by the obscure pictures on the front, and I studied the lyric sheets that sometimes came with them.

Mum had a Spanish guitar that her father had bought her whilst working in Columbia. Morfar was the managing director of a company that supplied the world with writing paper. It took him travelling everywhere, all around South America. He came back with some interesting things. The guitar was very unusual. Unfortunately it had become slightly battered and scratched due to my brother and I mistreating and squabbling over it when we were little. My brother was more interested in toy cars and marbles but would do anything to start a fight, so I had to share it with him until he got bored.

I was quite scruffy as a young kid. Most of the time, I wore all my brother's hand-me-downs which was ok because I spent so much time outdoors, getting dirty. I preferred to have my hair short but mum liked it shoulder length so she could put it in pig tails.

My real love and passion was music from as long back as I can remember. The guitar hung from the wall by the strap which was hand woven, black with red roses and gold stitching. By the time I had worked out how to drag a chair over to stand on and reach out to un-hook the guitar from the wall was when I began to form a relationship with it. The cat gut strings sounded mellow and warm; they had a certain texture about them which reminded me of dry spaghetti. The back of the body was a deep, dark red which when polished would shine enough to see my reflection. The keys were ivory, and I loved to turn them and hear the notes change. Mum would give me that knowing look when she would go to play it and it would be out of tune but she never forbade me to use it and when she gave me a diagram of some simple chord shapes there was no stopping me. I was addicted. That guitar was treated with a new kind of respect. It was no longer a toy, it was a friend.

A few years later it was noticed and taken seriously that I had a real interest in music. Whenever I went to people's houses I would look around for a guitar; I presumed every house had one. One day unexpectedly my dad came home from an auction in the village with an Epiphone Dreadnought. I was confused, I thought it must be for mum or someone else. It was in a grey soft case; he handed it over to me like it was no big deal, and my initial excitement was slightly numbed by disbelief but when I unzipped the case and saw the shiny unscratched wood and the sparkle of the steel strings, I felt like my new life had just begun. It wasn't my birthday or anything and we didn't have much money, but dad did that wonderful thing for me, and I was overjoyed. I was quite small, a slow developer and the guitar was huge, but I didn't care, I would grow into it. My parents watched as I tried a few chords but the pads on my fingers were soft from playing with gut strings. I took it up to my bedroom where it stayed out of reach of my brother and like a new friend, I got to know it slowly, gradually and with respect.

As a young girl I spent a lot of my spare time outside, climbing trees, making camps, catching pond life getting muddy in the garden either alone or with my brother or friends. We had rope swings, a tree house and a zip wire on our wooded, rugged, mud filled land; it was like an adventure playground, without health, safety and risk assessments. We got cut, bruised and scuffed but just got up and brushed ourselves off. Dad made a lake, he filled it with koi carp, we had a little wooden boat in there. The lake was clean enough and big enough to swim in.

The hours of fun were endless.

On a rainy day or when the sun went down, I would be chilling out inside within the comfort of an open log fire practising my guitar. Dad was a tree surgeon, fencer, logger, builder of anything wooden and good at making things for us kids. Home for me was muddy boots in the porch, chocolate cakes, dogs, parties, and lots of music.

The log cabin which my dad built.

Dad built a couple of log cabins at the bottom of the land. One was small but big enough to sleep in but the big one we used for parties; it was big enough to live in. They were built in the traditional Canadian way. My Grandmother lived independently in the cottage next door to our house but in the flat above lived her boyfriend, Kit. They were both very much in our lives. Gran was a very eccentric lady, bred Alsatians. She preferred dogs to people. Everyone loved gran but she had a side to her that was cold and hard. My mother saw that side on occasions, and so did I when I got older but to everyone else, she was wonderful. She saved birds, particularly owls when they were rescued from trees that my dad was cutting down. She had a spider monkey too which bit me badly, it wasn't tame and potentially dangerous so one day after it had escaped, running up the lane to the village it was advised that she had it put down. I was devastated as I saw it being shot in its cage whilst eating a banana. Gran also took in neglected, abused horses and had them fit and healthy again in no time. She was for sure a fascinating lady and I loved drinking tea with her and listening to her stories, but she had no real love for me and told me so one day. She adored my brothers and left her whole estate to them when she died. I was hurt at the time but not from a monetary point of view. I came to understand how important it is in life to treat people fairly; it prevents hostility and jealousy. I accepted her decision, it was totally her choice, and I don't begrudge anyone, but it could have easily put a wedge between the family. I don't think she could see the bigger picture at the time. She had several grandchildren, so I wasn't the only forgotten one.

My Grandfather on my father's side was also a remarkably interesting man, although I only ever saw him after church on a Sunday, wearing his robes and white collar. He wrote and prepared his own sermons; he was certainly a performer and a highly creative man too. He had many wartime stories, flying a Sopwith camel in the 1st world war which he'd been trained to fly by Malcolm Campbell at the age of 16. He later got shot down but unscathed and then spent time in a German prison camp on the Russian border. After the war he studied theology and became the Reverend of Hambleden church.

Grandad died when I was 10 and although I never really got to know him, I have always had an admiration for him and feel like we could have connected quite well on some levels. My father had a strict upbringing but that was the way back in those days and I feel that he carried it over to us children. He had a short temper and could behave in quite a manic way at times, but he was very charismatic and incredibly creative when it came to building things out of wood. Mum was calm and placid; she had an aura about her that people were drawn to. She was accepting and forgiving, I could tell her anything. My childhood, I feel was well balanced.

My grandfather Canon Wilfred Watts. When Edward V11 came to Hambleden church

All the colour

Through the rawness of my pain,

I find relief out in the rain,

the sky is crying with me, comforting me, aching just the same.

For a moment I see beauty in the way that love can change me, it can save me and destroy me, but it cannot kill my senses.

All the colour and the sunshine, all the smiles and the kisses

won't take away my tears and grant me all my wishes.

There is colour all around me, but it's hidden in the darkness, I can smell the grass, so sweet, the ground is soft beneath my feet.

The rain is tingling my cheeks, my heart is feeling very weak but there is colour all around me and I know that it surrounds me.

It is raining in my heart, and I am drowning in my sorrow,

help me make it through today, help me make it through tomorrow.

I am aching but I'm faking as I smile at the colours of the flowers and the beauty all around me and it's torturing me.

All the colour and the sunshine, all the smiles and the kisses

won't take away my tears and grant me all my wishes.

It's very difficult to describe in words the feeling of emotional pain. We've all felt it and there is always someone so much worse off but that doesn't make the pain less prevalent. It consumes you; it physically hurts and only time dilutes the rawness, but it never really goes away, we just learn to keep it in a box and hide it away so we can carry on with our lives. One day when I was feeling sick with grief, I made myself pick up the guitar just so I could hear what pain sounded like through an instrument and the tune was morosely sad but I found it comforting. It was raining outside and cold which I was grateful for so I went for a walk, without a coat so I could feel the physical discomfort which was also ironically comforting and the lyrics came to me, nothing poetically thought out, just truth. For me it was a way of processing the early stage of emotional pain when you don't know what to do with yourself.

From a young age I listened to Mum's records, working out the chords and lyrics to the songs. It was such a revelation to be able to sing and play something I'd only ever heard on a record. When I was busy learning music I was totally focused, I was in a time bubble, hours could pass that seemed like minutes. I could shut the world out and sometimes I had to. Later I discovered I had developed a tool to get me through some difficult and harrowing times. It worked for anxiety, fear, loneliness, and gut- wrenching emotional pain. Music became my comfort, my healer, and my saviour. They say things happen in threes so besides my mother's sudden illness we had two very tragic incidents that happened all within a year or two of each other. One night we had a serious fire that killed our dog, Sam. It happened before dawn one winter morning and I went to school that day feeling completely broken. The other incident occurred one Saturday night when my brother had a party. My parents had gone away for the weekend, and I stayed the night at my friend, Kirsty's house. When I returned home the next morning, I discovered that a boy was being pulled out of our lake. They had all gone swimming which resulted in the fatal accident.

I talk about those times because to me they were my defining moments that turned me from feeling obliviously safe and secure, to being almost terrified of everything and strangely unstable. I felt weak and fragile, expectant of disasters.

Through that weakness though I eventually found strength. I also found a deeper love for music. It was like I'd been stripped of my outer shell, naked and vulnerable so I looked inward to find my safe place and within that core was a whole new world of imagination and creativity; the anxiety dissipated, and the dreams would flow.

School didn't appeal to me except for the social aspect of it. The lessons bored me, I was un-enthused and frustrated. I struggled to take in information if it was uninteresting and couldn't concentrate or sit still for lengthy periods of time. My mind was active, but I would escape to that imaginary world of my own.

The shame I felt for not understanding things was destroying. I felt stupid, the teachers were frustrated with me, I'd get told off for not doing my maths and would sit in class trying not to cry. These days they call it dyspraxia. When I saw numbers, my head would be filled with jumbled up mess. My Dad would test us the times table every Sunday and I was ok with that if they were written down. We would sing or chant them in parrot fashion, and I would remember them, like learning lyrics to a song. If only teachers knew back then how some brains worked best. Learning through play makes perfect sense. How can you learn when you are bored?

Homework was soul destroying. The institution of school was one thing, a way of keeping children safe while parents went out to work, but home, I felt was my sanctuary, a place where I didn't want to feel guilt tripped and pressured to do something I strongly disliked. I blame school for making me feel inadequate. My parents never really knew whether I was studying. Apart from Sunday afternoon tests they left me to do my own thing. They knew I was mostly playing guitar, working out songs when in my room.

View of Malvern priory

Since moving to Malvern about 27 years ago most of the people I have met have been creative minded, eccentric characters. Everyone has a story and not afraid to tell it. The talent here is incredible. The pace of life is slower, houses are cheaper, and the people are very friendly.

Malvern is home to many writers, poets, and musicians. Edward Elgar, opera singer, Jenny Lind and Nigel Kennedy lived here. Ann (Charles Darwin's daughter) is buried in the Malvern priory graveyard where I like to sit and write and also CS Lewis studied at Malvern College. It certainly is a special place. I would say that Malvern allows you to be yourself and I, at the age of 53, am aiming to be the best version of me that I can be.

Growing up in Henley on Thames was a challenge at times, expectations were high, the pressure to achieve was too much but it gave me certain building blocks for what was coming later in my life. Henley taught me to be competitive. At least to try and make something of myself.

From about the age of five I was enrolled into the Henley children's theatre group where we were taught how to dance, act and sing. Twice a year we would do a show. Up until I was about 12 it took up my every Saturday, so I gave it up to free my weekends and hang out with friends in Henley or we'd get a bus to Reading. When I was 10 years old my drama coach, Flavia Pickworth, picked me and one other girl to audition in London for 'The sound of music'. It was extremely exciting. We had the week off school where our parents alternately drove us daily up to the Apollo theatre in London. My friend got the part as Brigitta Von Trapp which was incredible as thousands of children queued up daily along the streets of Westminster, desperate to be picked. I wasn't particularly disappointed, I knew I didn't have all the skills of a performer; when it came to dancing, I had two left feet. I was one of the few remaining though, as the queues and chaos thinned out. It was a fantastic experience that I'll never forget.

Our house where I grew up was about 3 miles from Henley. It was situated in a quiet remote area about a mile away from Shiplake station. I had many friends and a good social life. From 11 years onwards, I would hang out down at the station, a load of us, all ages. My brother Patrick and I would cycle there from our house. I would sometimes sit on the front of his BMX as he was quick, and we'd do it in about 8 minutes. Whatever the time, day or evening, there was usually someone there out of the Shiplake lot to talk to. I'd sit there for hours sometimes; it was like a youth club. We made our own entertainment as there wasn't much else to do.

Shiplake was a very middle class, affluent village by the river, about 5 mins by train to Henley. Home to a few famous rock stars. The prestige of the area didn't stop us rebellious youngsters being a nuisance at the station. The police were repeatedly called. Youth worker, Sarah, tried to set up a club for us on a Wednesday evening at the memorial hall. We went along but all it really achieved was a couple of hours' respite for the neighbours of Shiplake station.

My best friends at the time were Vicky and Kirsty. Vicky was like a sister. We first met at playgroup and were inseparable at primary school; we were known as Anna and Victoria, the terrible twins. We were quite bad at times, got into lots of trouble but then turned on the sweetness and put on shows for our parents. We were the singing, dancing, attention seeking duo that would stop at nothing to have fun. With help from my Mum Vicky and I started an annual tradition at Shiplake school that celebrated Santa Lucia. With candles in our hair, and ginger biscuits, singing the famous song to the whole of the school. As we got older, we pushed every boundary and got away with everything we could.

At 12 years we bunked off school, hitchhiked to London and busked Beatles songs in the underground. We looked older than 12, we'd change into jeans and t-shirts as soon as we were out of the vicinity of our homes. Whilst roaming the streets of London I remember being propositioned a few times by dodgy men. It was a dangerous time, but we couldn't see it, life was just one big adventure.

Whilst hitch hiking home, the second lift we got was a lady who knew our parents. She was nice and chatty, she didn't mention who she was and later that evening she called Vicky's and my Mum, and we ended up being grounded. We found ways to escape though. One night it was freezing cold and Vicky couldn't get back into her house as the window she'd crawled out of had been shut so the two of us wandered down the road and found a car down near the station that was unlocked. We crawled inside, curled up like spoons to keep warm, and waited, unable to sleep until the morning. We continued our adventures, ignoring the repercussions and took full advantage of our appeal and ability to charm. Throughout our childhood friendship, Vicky and I developed uncanny similarities. We dressed the same, had our hair the same and our voices were so similar that we could cover for each other on the phone if we had to. By the end of primary school our relationship remained tight, like sisters but we knew we had to allow ourselves to form close friendships with other people. We were put in different forms at Gillotts' which was good for us but the closeness between us was never lost.

Vicky and I on the boat in our pond.

Kirsty and I hit it off straight away. She lived in Shiplake, a 20-minute walk from mine. We discovered boys together, discos, smoking, Merrydown cider, and sneaking out at night. Kirsty's Dad, Zal, was in famous bands. He was an amazing guitarist, we used to go and watch him play in London and go backstage. I felt so privileged to have met some great celebrities. Kirsty and I both got into Buddy Holly music together after watching the Buddy Holly Story. We watched it so many times that we knew the script inside out. That music became the soundtrack of my years at Gillotts school. I liked other music but found it hard to be inspired by the 80's electronic stuff that had begun and was really taking off. My friend and next-door neighbour across the field, Tom, became one of the Chemical Brothers. I had no idea when we were kids that he had this incredible, creative other side to him. Living in an area where there was a rock star virtually on every street made me even more determined to pursue a career in music one day, but I was too painfully shy to try to do it on my own. I wouldn't even sing in front of my parents.

I was desperate to put a band together. I tried but none of my friends were as into it as me. I was no singer but loved the guitar and young as I was, I loved writing songs. The first song I wrote was about being in prison. I had a vivid imagination. I remember describing the cell in detail. I still have an image of it now, although in my mind's eye at the time it was in the basement of Henley town hall. As a child I used to walk past and see the iron bars at ground level and imagine that people were locked up in there. The tune I wrote was very melancholic. I was learning how to finger pick the guitar strings and was fascinated by minor chords.

I sent the song off to 'Saturday morning superstore super star' which was a TV competition. I recorded it on one of those basic square tape decks, popped it in the post with the lyrics handwritten, a picture of me and a brief description of myself. I didn't expect a reply but kept checking the post box anyway. A few weeks later once I'd given up all hope, a letter arrived for me. They loved it! I was invited to an audition in London. I was so excited. My lyrics had been read and my recording had been listened to. I tried to get Vicky and another friend, Athol, to start up a trio so I wouldn't have to do it on my own. Athol, son of 60's singer, song writer, Vince Hill played the drums and had a music room at the top of his Jacobean Riverside mansion. Mum had some great ideas, she suggested we call ourselves

'The convicts' and wear overalls with arrows on. I organised rehearsals but the two of them messed about, they didn't take it as seriously as me. It got awfully close to the date, and we weren't ready. I was totally unprepared and far too shy to audition on my own, so it failed to happen.

I had some great friends in Henley. Growing up. Most of them were quite sporty and academic. I struggled to fit in with the clever ones. I wanted to be more like them with their organised pencil cases and smartly covered exercise books but the more I tried the more disappointed I became in myself. My school bag was a mess. Half-eaten sandwiches, dog eared books and my bulldozer shoes that my parents made me wear to school; of course I would change out of them. They were practical and would last forever but there was no way I was going to be seen in them. It was a good 10-minute walk to the bus stop down a pot holed lane, jumping over puddles. The backs of my legs would get splattered with mud. I'd get to the bus stop, brush my tights down and swap my brown leather bull dozers for my low healed navy-blue stilettos.

Academically I failed to achieve. My schoolwork was poor, not just maths, everything. I was always being sent to the headmaster for bad reports. After a while the constant criticism and reprimanding destroyed my confidence and I later became vulnerable to bad influences like smoking and bunking off school. I have no regrets though. Some of my best times were jumping on a BMX with a bunch of lads just before a maths lesson and pedalling out the back way, through the woods, over jumps and downtown with big grins on our faces. That feeling of freedom and rebelliousness was addictive and empowering. We often had to face tough consequences but usually we got away with it by forging sick notes.

I was in the lower sets for maths and English and my peers were disruptive. No one paid attention. To be seen working was detrimental to your social status within the class so I learned to fit in and do as little as possible.

Mr Perrim was short and quite chubby, with a ruddy complexion. He taught me English and music in the fifth year and saw something in me those other teachers didn't. He chose me and my good friend, Kate, to do the opera workshop which involved a week off school, training and performing with the London royal opera society. Kate and I had turned every English and music lesson into a comedy show for the rest of the class with our silly antics. Mr. Perrim thought we had creative flair rather than being naughty, so he allowed us to channel it into something more productive, so we got a small part in Carmen. Every day was exciting, training and rehearsing. Mr Perrim had given us that opportunity and great experience. If only there had been more teachers like him.

I grew up feeling embarrassed about my ambitions. They were considered by a lot of people as indulgent fantasies, unreachable goals and to be kept as a hobby. To live in Henley, you needed to work towards a proper career, a trade, or qualifications as the cost of living there was so high.

I left school at 16 with one O level which was art. I was properly ashamed of myself. The only course for me at college was parent craft. They wouldn't even allow me the opportunity to retake my exams. This decision was made by one teacher at college who interviewed me. She must have spent a mere 5 minutes reading my school report and decided I had learning difficulties and would never manage an O level course. I didn't explain my home situation with mum's illness and how I'd missed so many lessons. I had too much dignity to use that card. I felt humiliated and incredibly stupid. My parents must have been at a complete loss as to what to do with me. I had to get a job that's all there was to it.

It was the middle of a recession and I had to decide what to do with my life. Jobs were scarce. Through an Aunt I was given a number to call about a job as a live-in nanny. I called and got an interview. Dressed in a summer frock I went along to meet the family and introduce myself. There were two grown up kids, my age and a two-year-old. The grown-up kids were college students. The little boy, Tom, was adorable. The parents seemed nice, and they liked me, so it was a done deal. I had a job and a place to live. They had a summer house in Cornwall where we spent 6 weeks of the summer. The older kids came too. The family was great. They gave me days off and I was included in all the social events. At night all the youngsters in the village sat in the sand dunes with beers. I took my guitar and got everyone singing around a campfire made from driftwood. It was a memorable time. After the summer things changed, the kids went to college and I was lonely. I stuck it out for a few months but looked out for another job where I could live at home. The family I worked for were very understanding and even helped me job hunt.

After many failed interviews I was accepted as a trainee dental nurse. Not at all what I wanted to do but I desperately needed a job. The high-pitched sound of aspirators, the smell of burning rotten teeth and abscesses repelled me. I stuck it out for a while on minimum wage. I suppose you could say it was character building, but I was so unhappy and dreaded it every day. The dentists were tyrants, I got shouted at constantly for not being quick enough. Sitting on the bus at 7am on a winter's morning, picking the scabs on my scalp that had appeared through stress and wishing the week to end, was what made me realise I had to change my life. It was a long shot, but I phoned Henley college and explained how I had applied to retake my O levels the previous year and been turned down. They invited me in for a chat. It was a different woman. She asked me all about myself and I filled her in. I told her about my year working and explained how and why I struggled at school. She asked me about my hobbies and passions and together we chose a course of subjects that suited me. I enrolled to do 5 AS levels which was a year's course and decided to pay attention and work hard. I did art, photography, drama, media studies and human biology. I came out with 2 grade C's and 3 B's.

The best thing that came out of that year in college was knowing that I wasn't stupid, I just wasn't academic. There at college I met my first love, Dan. He was a guitarist too. We became best friends. He had long straight fair hair and was into heavy metal bands. Our music interests clashed a bit but apart from that we had a lot in common. After a couple of years our lives went in different directions. Dan went to art college, and I needed to start working again. Our friendship groups changed, we had little time to spend together, and we started arguing over silly things. It was time to explore other avenues.

I found a job as a paste up artist in a t-shirt printing factory. I had the required qualifications but there were over 100 people applying for it. I wanted it badly and read up all about screen printing, blagged the interview and got it!

The company was based in Reading, my job involved graphics, design, and colour separation for the silk screens. It was an 8am start. Quite a big responsibility and hard work but I loved it, and my colleagues were great. My brother's best friend, James Bristow, worked in Reading so gave me a lift to and from work most days. He had an old white Rover. With his elbow out the window, he would rock up at 7.30am with Rod Stewart, blasting out on the stereo. He drove too fast and through Caversham he would cut up the one-way street the wrong way to avoid the traffic jams. Life was good. I began to like myself. Work was brilliant, I had my own office and dark room, the people were great but best of all I got to do artwork every day. I designed logos and t-shirts for bands as well as big companies.

James Bristow.

Music was no longer at the forefront of my brain. I put all my creative energy into my work. I was still living at home and paying my parents rent. Mum was ok, she was having regular check-ups, but she was suffering with epilepsy due to scar tissue on the brain. It worried me a lot as I would come home sometimes and find her unconscious. It always looked so much worse than it actually was, but it never failed to terrify me.

One day mum and dad decided to move up to Wales. Dad got onto a forestry course at Bangor university in Wales following a serious accident where he fell 50 foot out of a tree. He had been in hospital for weeks recovering from broken vertebrae in his spine. It was touch and go as to whether he could do physical work again, so the idea was to get a degree and do consultancy work instead. They initially rented the family home out to my brother, Patrick and me; then we found 3 others to share the rent with us, Patrick's girlfriend Les, my friend, Kate, and one other whom we selected after putting an advert out for a room available. Her name was Kay. We met her once and the decision was unanimous. A nurse in a psychiatric ward, a little older than us, but friendly and responsible. She had prematurely grey hair, which was thick and coarse. She kept it short and spikey in a slightly punky style. Her clothes were mainly purple, and she had several tattoos. It was a few weeks before I started seeing signs that Kay was a little strange. She painted her room purple and put purple silk scarfs over the lamp shades. The smell of her Joss sticks dominated the house. I got on alright with her at first, but I figured out over the weeks that something didn't quite add up. To begin with, everything was normal. She left at 8 am every day to go to work and was home in the evening. She later revealed that she had a daughter who was going to start visiting every Saturday.

The little girl would arrive with a lady who I assumed was a family member. Whenever I broached the subject about her daughter though, Kay would turn and dismiss it. She refused to talk about her. It wasn't many weeks in before Kay started staying at home during the day or disappearing for days on end and I was concerned that she had lost her job. When questioned she would get cross. Eventually we had a call from the hospital where she supposedly worked asking if Kay was alright because she hadn't been going in. We were obviously quite concerned too as our rent money was due. It turned out that she wasn't a nurse at the hospital, but a day patient and she had various mental illnesses.

We continued to allow her to stay and she made the monthly payments and all was ok until one day when I was in the bathroom and she repeatedly banged on the door, shouting through in an overly aggressive, manic way. Hurriedly I finished washing and opened the door to her. She squared right up to me, threatening to kill me. Her words confused me as she growled into my face incoherently. I shook like a leaf and tried to calm her, apologising for whatever I might have done to upset her, but she wouldn't back down; it was like she was on a drug induced psychotic trance. She left the house that morning and I explained to everyone else what had happened, but they slept through it and assumed that she was just in a bad mood. It was more than getting out of bed the wrong side and I wanted her gone. It wasn't as simple as that though. She was ill and we couldn't kick her out on the street, so I left that day. My friend, Kate, followed shortly afterwards. We moved into a friend's shared house in Henley. It wasn't ideal but it was safe. We knew the lads that lived there, Steve, Jon and Jo and there was a room going that Kate and I could share. It wasn't easy but it was certainly a memorable experience. The lads played tricks on us every day and expected us to do all the housework. There was no heating, and it was always a mess, dirty dishes, overflowing bins, bodies sprawled around the living room and parties every night. I would start my day with two cups of coffee and a Pro Plus before heading to work.

I met Evan at one of our house parties. He was always the last to leave and regularly slept on the couch. He was painfully thin with chestnut brown shoulder length hair and various badly designed tattoos on his back, legs, and arms. He often borrowed cash off me as he was unemployed. All the signs were there to not get involved but I was attracted to his rebellious character and sense of humour. He was several years older than me and had a certain authority about him. His confidence and experience of life was one of the things that appealed to me. He was charming in a laddish kind of way and stood out to me amongst the boys I'd been with as more of a man. Very soon we were in a steady relationship. I struggled to feel at ease with him from the start though as he seemed so much more mature, and I was so less confident than him which strangely made the relationship even more appealing.

In the mornings before leaving for work I would make him coffee and hand him a few pounds to get him through the day, but he'd doze back off to sleep. It wasn't unusual for him to still be lying there on the sofa when I returned from work.

I phoned in sick on a couple of occasions as encouraged by Evan and it wasn't long before I started losing focus on my job. I was tired from the late-night parties. I made mistakes and turned up late on occasions and none of this went unnoticed. Evan introduced me to marijuana. He rolled joints and smoked them all day like they were cigarettes. My friend, Kate, and I got into smoking it too after work, it made us lazy and unmotivated.

Staring into the flame

My Mother's illness was the catalyst that changed everything. I noticed her confusion during regular phone calls. She thought I was still at school even though I sent her t-shirts that I'd designed at work. Dad was still at university but struggling to concentrate with his studies as well as Mum's decline. She had been suffering on and off for about 5 years. During my mocks at secondary school, she was having a big tumour removed from her brain followed by a long bout of radio therapy. I had to take time off, my younger brother was only about 6 at the time, and I needed to help with him. She did get better for a while and was in remission but later it returned.

Struggling a bit with my job at the T-shirt factory and with failed negotiations about my promised pay rise made me consider whether it was time to re-evaluate my future. I was worried sick about Mum, she was starting to forget who I was when I called. I couldn't focus on work, I was confused, nobody could explain what was happening. I had to find out, I had to leave my job. I went to Wales to be with her. I know I left it a little too late as by the time I got there she was even getting worse by the day. Initially Evan came with me, but it all got too much. I had no time for him, he started arguing with me about ridiculous things. I had spent all my overdraft and couldn't afford to buy him tobacco or beer, so he left to go back to sofa surfing and just visited me on the odd occasion.

My little brother, Daniel, was happy to see me. They were living in the grounds of a big derelict stately home near Bangor, close to his university.

They had a small cottage, once used by the groundsmen. There wasn't a spare room there for me, so I made a cosy space in one of the wings of the big house. It was a bit musty and very run down but all I needed was a room for myself and Evan when he visited. In the room was a king size bed and huge bay windows looking out onto a run down, out of use but beautiful old water fountain. I borrowed clean sheets and blankets from the cottage. I had running water, electricity, and a kettle, I was sorted. It was the end of summer, the weather was still quite warm but winter was not far away, so I stocked up on rum, roll ups and snacks with the rest of my overdraft. It wasn't ideal being in Wales but it was where I had to be, close to Mum and there for Daniel who needed me. On occasions when Evan wasn't there, Daniel would stay the night at mine; we called it the squat. I would get the rum out, play guitar and sing to him. His favourite song was 'Streets of London'. To this day he still asks me to sing it. I was a major fan of Ralph McTell. I loved his style of finger picking and his story telling lyrics.

Daniel was the bravest little boy I knew. He would try and hide his tears from us, but I would find him often under the bed or behind a door in the foetal position, silently sobbing, missing our Mum. It was heart wrenching to see. Our mother wasn't the same. The confusion had turned to complete cognitive impairment as her brain rapidly swelled and filled with fluid.

It is strange how we cope in these situations; we adapt through our inner strength and find new ways to relate to that person. You become their carer so the love changes. It was like we had swapped roles, the years that I had been nurtured and parented had taught me how to do the same for her, quite naturally. I laughed at the funny things she said in her state of confusion, encouraged and praised her efforts to eat, hold a cup, swallow her medication etc. I saw the odd sparkle in her eyes, a small reminder that she was in there still. When I sang to her or played a tune on my guitar, her fingers or toes would move just a little bit and a tear might roll down her cheek. She communicated in the most subtle ways that were only really noticeable to us but we learned to read her, knew what she needed and what would upset her. She loved having her hair washed and blow dried, it was long and silky. I would brush it gently until she dozed off to sleep.

Daniel needed mum so desperately but put the needs of us before his own, keeping us strong. Entertaining us with his jokes and playful humour. He spent his pocket money on gifts for Dad to try and cheer him up. Daniel really needed us, and we didn't consider him as much as we should have. He concealed his pain well.

On that fateful day when we watched Mum slip away, it was kind of a relief. She was really starting to suffer, and it was painful to see. It wasn't a peaceful departing though, it was traumatic in every way, and we waited for her last breath, for the pain to end. She died in the ambulance on the way to the hospital. Afterwards we lit a candle in her room in the cottage as we were told it would keep her spirit there. We kept it burning for 3 days.

I have a photo album that mum put together when Daniel was a baby. It was one of those albums that has a space for writing something next to each picture. Mum was always taking photos of us all with her little Kodak camera, and when Daniel was born, she was endlessly snapping away. I keep that album treasured, not just because of the pictures but because of the familiar writing in blue biro, her handwriting was very distinctive as were her words. When I look at that album now, I run my fingers over the script, I feel her presence and hear her voice. I'd like to think that one day my children will do the same when they read this book.

I wrote a song for Mum.

I am not religious but open minded and quite spiritual, I think. Writing this song several years after Mum had gone was during one of those moments when I felt her there in spirit. Even though she is not there in the physical sense, she has helped me through some lonely nights. Writing is like therapy for me, my way of releasing something inside me. I pick up my guitar which feels like a comforting friend within my arms and the strings will sound out the emotion that I'm feeling at the time. The guitar is like a channel that links my thoughts to the outside world. When I feel deeply connected with no outside distraction, the words and the tune come out without using any deliberate thought process. It's a magical feeling; it heals the soul.

This song is for mum...

'Staring into the flame' Staring into the flame
I see your face
You haven't changed
You still look the same
I wonder, can you hear me, When I call your name?
I wonder do you ever feel the pain?
Do you dry the tears
Like the sun dries the rain?

I see your face in the pattern on the wall I know it's you when you slam the door Are you near me?
Sometimes I hear your voice when I sleep,
and I feel your touch. Can you feel me?
Or is it all in my mind?
When the birds fly away
Do you leave this world behind?

Are you the wind that howls in the night?
Are you the star that shines so bright?
Are you the glow in the fire light?

Staring into the flame
I see your face
You haven't changed
You still look the same
In the dark you are my light.
You help me through the lonely nights.
Can you hear me?
Is it all in my mind?
Do you lead the way?
Are you giving me signs?

The lyrics of this song poured out one winter evening as I sat with a glass of wine watching the fire burn.

People ask me how I write. Do I put down the lyrics or the tune first...?

I don't have a consistent answer as there is no rule. If the song is meant to be, it will just flow. The tune and lyrics to this song came together simultaneously.

The lyrics are already there I suppose in the sub conscious, the sentiment makes the tune.

Dad had met a French lady during the last few months of Mum's life. He was open about his companionship with her, and I was happy that he had someone to keep him strong. It was a very surreal time. Dad was pale, thin, and completely exhausted. Conventional medicine was not working for Mum, so he tried alternative therapies. It was clear in the end that we had to accept that the fight was over, and we needed to let her go.

Dad and his new companion grew close, they needed each other. She was good for him. One day they decided to leave the country with my little brother, to live in France.

Little man.

In life you meet many people, those who come and go, acquaintances, soul mates, kindred spirits, buddies, colleagues, partners, first loves, the list goes on. You meet people that can define you, undermine you or leave impressions that are like an imprint on your soul, they never really go away. Good impressions or bad, they are there at the back of your mind, never forgotten. I also believe whether through nature or nurture there are those who control and those who are controlled, and the latter attracts the former. The controller is usually insecure and possessive. They have the type of imagination that runs away with them, always thinking irrationally and believing the worst. The one that's controlled is often shy, the child that sits alone, easily spotted by the confident one who steps in and befriends them. It is difficult to break that cycle and so it continues.

Evan made an impression on my life; I survived to tell the story and write the song. It was an experience that made me wiser and more understanding about relationships and how difficult it can be to walk out of one however dangerous or toxic it may be.

This song 'little man' is on our album 'Lost for words'. BBC Hereford and Worcester loved it, it became our signature song which was played as background music when they were introducing Hennesea and other songs. We rarely sing it live anymore. It needed to be written though, it's like cleaning the fur out of the crevices of the mind. Very satisfying.

'Little man'

The man she met when she was low and needed someone strong
Was not Mr Right but definitely Mr Wrong.
He led her down a bumpy road of misery and squalor
Amidst his pity looking shifty, He would sit and wallow

Little man, little man
Swigging from his can
Whose life is he destroying now?
Whose mind is he twisting and body molesting while his sorrow he is trying to drown?

When she looked into his eyes
All she saw was his disgrace
And the way he felt about her
Which was nothing but distaste.
What she didn't know
Was only he, he despaired
And he took it out on the one thing That he loved.

She made her getaway one day
When she was feeling strong
All the while thinking she was doing something wrong.
No more would she let him tread her soul into the ground.
So, she packed her bags and left Without a sound.
Little man, little man, swigging from his can.
Whose life is he destroying now?

Life was a mess, my family was broken, there was no pillar to keep it standing. The safe walls around me crumbled. After the initial shock, relief and stages of grief that goes with losing someone, the feuds started. We were all hurt, angry, bitter and sad. We said wrong things and made poor decisions.

I had no money, I was unemployed and homeless. To make matters worse I became captive to Evan and his controlling behaviour. He became aggressive towards me. People will say I had a choice, but I really felt I didn't. My father said I was blindly in love with him, that was the first time I'd heard that expression. Evan was toxic, I was young, lost and incredibly insecure about myself. He was all I believed I had, and I was, just like Dad had said, blindly in love with him. My older brother and my friends all knew that I was being mistreated but I became good at hiding it, covering up bruises and defending him. He had a side to his character that I protected, I wanted to help him. He had been abandoned at birth and endured a tough childhood. He needed someone to believe in him. I believed that with my help things would get better. I thought It was clear that Evan loved me, he was always devastated after losing his temper. I later realised that he was incapable of feeling real love.

What he had was an unhealthy obsession with me, a sense of ownership. He cleverly picked away at me, putting me down, ridding me of my own self, until eventually I didn't know who I was. Subsequently I became his possession.

The two of us stayed and slept on the floor of a friend's house; his friend, Ben. We didn't do much besides taking drugs and drinking too much alcohol. Speed was easily obtainable and there was always lots of marijuana about.

Day after day we sat in the smoke-filled sitting room of the shared house, curtains drawn, tv on, whilst listening to loud music. I had a diet of toast and tea. I was never hungry though.

I rarely played guitar; I was numb. Had I felt some kind of emotion I might have felt inspired to write.

Life was dull, I just smoked and drank to escape reality. Staying there was only temporary as we could not pay rent. I had a part time job in a pub which didn't pay much. Evan would do the odd illegal job but his money went straight on a drug purchase. He never explained what it was he was doing but would be out all night and return in the morning with a substantial amount of money. I never really questioned things. When he had his supply of recreational drugs, he was mostly happy and nice to me.

Things were not always predictable. Evan had deep rooted problems. I had started working at a Chinese restaurant in Henley. It was very upmarket, I got to meet many celebrities including one of our regulars, George Harrison. It was a decent job. I worked from 6pm till midnight most evenings, serving wine and washing up. After work we would all eat together and one of the staff members would drive me home. Evan and I had moved into the log cabin that my dad had built. He had sold the family house on the land, but my grandmother still had her cottage. The house was separated with its own piece of garden and fenced off. The rest of the land still belonged to gran. The cabin remained and Dad told me that I could stay in there if I wanted or needed to. It was basic but we made it liveable and kept it warm with the wood we collected. It became our home for a while. Evan wanted to start his own business, sand blasting so I helped him put a plan together to get a bank loan. He stayed on the straight and narrow for a while, avoiding drugs and alcohol. It wasn't easy for him, but I was proud of his efforts. I was doing ok too, enjoying my job at the restaurant.

Me in the log cabin that Dad built. My 21ˢᵗ birthday.

Things were looking up until one night when I came home late from work. It had been a busy night, I was exhausted. Evan had been waiting up for me. I walked in and noticed his eyes were black and piercing. He was shouting at me. I barely had time to speak and explain why I was late when the accusations started, followed by aggressive violence. Furiously filling the bath with water, he dragged me by the hair and tried to drown me. I fought with every bit of strength I had, loosened myself from his grip and tried to escape but he stopped me and started biting my fingers and scalp and kicking me repeatedly in my shins until they were bruised. Finally, he stopped. I was reduced to a broken, withering mess. He fell asleep on the bed whilst I sat on the cold wooden floor. My tears ran dry.

Often there were no tears, just a sick feeling in the pit of my stomach. I had faced worse things.

He woke up hours later. I don't know if he'd been drinking or what he'd taken but his words in the morning when he saw me were of someone in complete disbelief and shock, he genuinely seemed not to remember a thing about the previous night and wept for hours. I told him I was going to leave him, but he begged me not to and swore it would never happen again. I believed him.

As humans we tend not to use our instincts as much as we should. Even though we might have reservations, unexplained doubts, and feelings, we put those aside and look at other things like presentation, charm, mannerisms etc. We get drawn in by good looks, humour and generosity and ignore that niggling feeling, that first impression, that scent, our intuition.

I wrote this song having found a diary of mine where I had jotted down thoughts and feelings while I was in Greece. When I read those words many years later, I was immediately transported back in my mind to a time when my feelings were very raw. I had my pen and diary at hand with my head down trying to distract myself from the predators around me and hoping that they would see I wasn't interested and go away.

⸺◈⸺

Chapter 2

Telling me lies.

Telling me lies:

It took some time to realise

That place was cold as ice

The people all appeared very nice

But I could see the truth in their eyes

They were telling me, telling me, telling me, telling me lies

They were hiding, hiding, hiding behind their disguise.

The men I grew wary of, all were the same, some of them glared at me head hung in shame,

Sitting alone in a world of my own, minding my business, nobody's interested in what I say, or the songs that I play but I know I'll no longer be running, running away.

My soul I could not give but I lost the will to live, my mind was all that I had, and my mind was not all that bad,

I knew they were telling me lies.

They were hiding, hiding, hiding behind their disguise.

The stench of cheap whiskey on breath hot and frisky flashing their cash at me, wildly harassing me, lust-stricken eyes, greedy and wide,

I look for a place, a place I can hide.

I mind my own business nobody's interested in what I say or the songs that I play but I know I'll no longer be running, running away. I know I'll no longer be running, running away.

One day Evan and I decided to sell some belongings. He couldn't get a loan so the business plan didn't work out and we wanted to get away so we scraped together enough money to buy air tickets to Greece and escape the cold, wet English climate. Above all we wanted to escape the people that tried to break us up. People refused to understand what I saw in Evan. My best friend, Vicky, came over once and tried to talk some sense into me. That day was all a bit of a blur, but it resulted in Evan holding a knife to my throat and demanding she stayed out of my life. It was an impossible situation as I was fully committed to him and anyone that interfered with our relationship became the enemy. It sounds ridiculous to me now.

Leaving Henley felt like the right thing to do. I left my job and we fled to the island of Rhodes. I wasn't too worried about how we were going to survive. It was warm there and we had each other. The holiday season was about to start and pretty soon, sure enough we found work. For a while things were good, it was an adventure and exciting at first. Evan and I charmed our way around the small coastal town. Everything felt like it was turning out perfectly. We worked hard, saved hard and kept ourselves off the drugs. I didn't miss the cabin or the life of getting stoned in dark, smoky rooms. Evan struggled though. He missed his friends, his illegal dealings and his adrenaline fuelled heists with his partner in crime.

The novelty of our new life soon wore off and the abuse started again, emotionally as well as physically. It's the emotional abuse that sticks in my mind. The mental torment scarred me, reducing me to become a pathetic weak human with no self-esteem.

We worked for several months in a taverna, Evan in the kitchen pot washing, I was out front serving drinks. I respected the fact that it wasn't pleasant for him in the sweat box of a kitchen with the occasional cockroach crawling up his bare legs, but he hated that I was behind the bar chatting to Greeks and appearing to be flirting with the young male staff.

Some nights after work we would sit outside with the other staff, drinking beer and eating pizza. I was always asked to get my guitar out which I kept safe behind the bar, and we would sing songs until dawn. Evan made fun of me in many ways and continuously put me down but when it came to music, he fully encouraged me. He talked about being my manager and tried getting me gigs but when it came down to it people would take one look at him and shake their heads with disapproval. He looked menacing and untrustworthy to some people with the hard, cold expression in his eyes and very visible tattoos. He had a stance about him like he was ready to pounce. Years of watching his own back. He had crossed many people, but he also had an in-built fight or flight mechanism from growing up having to defend himself against the harsh world he was born into.

One evening Evan cried off work, he was exhausted and fed up, he'd been working hard for weeks, and I was proud of him. For that, he deserved a break, so he went out into town with some biker chaps that he met in the bar the night before. When he returned the following day after I had been worrying all night, he had lost all our savings. He told me he had been mugged. We argued a little, but I think he'd taken something, he mentioned a pill, but he didn't know what it was. He was calm and a little lucid, he didn't get aggressive, but I needed answers. I'd worked for months saving up. All he could say to me was that he needed to go back to England.

The taverna we worked in was in a small village near the airport. Our boss had friends who worked there so made a phone call to the airport manager and on that very same day Evan got a spare free seat on the plane flying back to Heathrow. I decided to stay on Rhodes until the end of the season, it was still fairly busy, and they needed me. I ran the bar pretty much on my own and knew exactly what everyone's tipple was and how they liked it served and presented. Surprisingly Evan was fine about me staying, he knew he'd done wrong; he was like a dog with his tail between his legs.

I was relieved when he got on that plane as he was starting to get irritated and fractious. He was using emotional abuse to hurt me again. He knew how to really push that knife in. He could never take back those words, they hung around my neck and pulled me down, sometimes so low it's a wonder I could ever stand up straight again.

I needed that break. I knew that our relationship wasn't over though, I was trapped like a rabbit in a snare, and I understood I would have to face him again soon.

Being so alone and vulnerable in a foreign country left me wide open to exploitation. I had little self-esteem, I was naive, in a place where women were treated like second class citizens. If you were young and fair, you were prey. Every man I met had an agenda, very few men were genuinely kind to me, and I needed kindness and protection. With Evan I was not allowed to grieve the death of my mother, I was never encouraged to talk about her and if I did, I was urged to keep it to myself.

Alone in Greece with no money and a job that paid extremely little was a recipe for disaster. I became the target for demanding power headed men. It later became clear to me that it was not luck that Evan got a free flight home, somebody had made that happen for their own selfish reasons. A man I respected and saw like a father figure used this opportunity to really cross the line. He was overweight with white balding hair in his mid 50's. He had groomed me over the months and built up my trust just to abuse it. That man was my boss. Going for an after-work drink didn't seem so strange. He used to let me drive his Sierra Cosworth into town for cigarettes most nights after work, him in the passenger seat instructing me as I didn't have a licence. We would then go back to the restaurant and drink whiskey. I shared with him some of my darkest stories.

On this one night after Evan had gone home, we went to a bar in town. It was quiet at work, so we closed the bar early. I trusted him and thought it would be a pleasant thing to do having worked hard all through the summer without a single night off. I had a white wine and we chatted. We sat in a quiet corner of a pretty taverna which had vine leaves hanging down from above. I remember that clearly as a branch was tickling the back of my neck. My boss chose to sit beside me instead of opposite which made me feel a little uncomfortable. The wine tasted good, and I slurped it down a little too fast, but I was quite a hardened drinker and I felt fine. That's the last thing I remember about that evening in the taverna.

Sometime later that evening I woke up, disoriented, lying in the back seat of my boss's car, he was on top of me. I realised what he was trying to do so I fought him off and hurled myself out onto what felt like sand beneath me. It was dark and I could hear the waves. I started to vomit, my head was spinning, I was confused. I had no idea where I was and I was dizzy and weak. He was flattering me with words that made me want to throw up again. I was silent in the car, I felt violated. There is no way I had allowed that situation to happen. I don't even know what happened, but he was grinning like a cat that got the cream.

That night left me feeling even more worthless. Confronting him or telling anyone was not an option. He was a married man and well respected in the community, also he was on first name terms with the police. My story was too weak, I felt guilty and ashamed. I packed my bag as soon as I awoke the next morning, dehydrated, a banging headache and very nauseous. There were details of that night which I remember clearly but the rest is completely blank.

I had no one to call except for Evan and I couldn't tell him what had happened. I asked him to try and find me some money to get home. He said he'd sort it, but it would take about a week. I realised I had to survive on nothing until then. I couldn't stay on Rhodes after what had happened, so I went to the airport to try and get an empty seat on a flight. I found someone from the management team, someone I recognised from dining in the Taverna, and he invited me into his office. He was tall, thin, middle aged with greying hair. He seemed friendly, and I felt at ease asking him if there were any spare seats going. He sat me down in his office, asked me how I was and what I thought of Greece and the usual small talk, but I just needed that ticket, and I couldn't stress enough how urgent it was. A look came over his slightly wrinkled, weathered face, he shifted his spectacles, squinted his eyes, and said he would like to take me for dinner to discuss it. That was when the alarm bells went. I suddenly felt unsafe again, embarrassed, stupid, and enraged by the idea of being coerced into doing something I didn't want to do. A favour for a favour. There was no genuine kindness. I felt so humiliated and couldn't get out of that airport quick enough. I left with that familiar feeling of frustration and disappointment. Emotional pain had been building up inside me and the trigger had just been pulled.

It felt good to cry, I don't know what I was crying about, there were too many things. I had to be strong though. I had to wipe away the tears, hold my head up and lose that vulnerability that kept getting me into trouble. It would not be easy, but I had to survive.

Lonesome dream.

'I'm a survivor'

These three words got me through some tough times.

I was still learning and still making mistakes, wrong decisions, and bad choices. I could survive a week with no money, what was there to fear? As long as I avoided men, kept my head down and stayed strong. I had my guitar, the beach, open air markets where I could pinch the odd bread stick or banana. I could sleep rough, the nights weren't too cold. I just needed to toughen up a bit, get creative, find shelter, try and stay safe.

Lonesome dream.

Green is the grass that I see on the other side and I'm going to find my dream,

Long is the road that I walk on my own but when I get there, I know I will be free.

Free, but it ain't easy, what I'm going to I cannot foresee,

Me, I'm a survivor and I'm living a lonesome dream.

White are the streetlights, black is the cold night and I'm running to keep myself warm,

Red is the sunrise, blue is the morning sky and I smile to the beauty of the dawn

I'm free but it ain't easy, what I'm going to I cannot foresee,

Me, I'm a survivor and I'm living a lonesome dream.

Gold is the warm sand, silver is the ocean

and I lay my head, listen to the seagull's cry,

then in my mind I can see my reflection,

there are shadows like dark circles around my eyes

But I'm free and it ain't easy, what I'm going to I cannot foresee,

Me I'm a survivor and I'm living a lonesome dream.

Feeling positive I jumped aboard the boat to Piraeus, the mainland Greece. I would have to hide from the ticket collector but was told that was easy enough. I stayed out on deck and moved around whenever I saw him, he was easy to spot in his uniform. It was an 8-hour trip and people boarded from every island on the way to the mainland, so tickets were being constantly inspected. A few hours into the trip I got caught and was told to get off at the next island, Leros. I got chatting to a Greek truck driver who was delivering building supplies to Leros and he knew people that lived there.

The island of Leros was infamous at the time for its prison for psychiatric patients. 'The colony of psychopaths' was what the Greeks called it. Most people that lived there had connections to the prison, either builders or staff. It was not known as a destination for holiday makers which in a way made it even more beautiful and fascinating. It did intrigue me, however, as to how the ticket man on the boat thought it would be right to force me to disembark on Leros knowing the situation there at that time which I'd heard was shocking.

We arrived at the port, and I climbed into the passenger seat of the truck. We drove a short distance to a taverna where several people, all Greek, sat outside, eating, drinking and playing tavli which is their version of backgammon. The trucker seemed to know everyone there and introduced me to his friend, a short chubby man with the familiar salt and pepper dusted scalp, of a middle-aged Greek. He reminded me of Danny DeVito. They shook hands and exchanged a few words and shortly after that the truck driver said goodbye to me and left. He told me that I was in good hands, and I could stay safely with that man.

So, there I was taking a gamble on the situation, trusting what was in front of me, knowing things could go terribly wrong but I had no choice. It was a toss between that or sleeping rough and given that the island was home to many thousands of psychopaths in an over populated, under staffed, poorly run prison I chose to stick with the Danny DeVito guy.

It took a lot for me to feel anything like the pain I had already endured over the years. One thing I had though was a good mind, I knew right from wrong, and my instincts were becoming quite highly tuned. I wasn't scared really but something felt so very wrong about the last night in Rhodes. How can I trust myself if I can black out like that after one drink? A quiet drink after work with someone, a married man, my boss, whom I thought I could rely on, resulting in confusion, memory loss and a deep sense of violation. It was all out of my control which was a bit scary.

I was wary of every man, yet I was still being led by their false generosity. What else could I do? I could run if I had to, fast, and I could fight. I was fit enough but I would not allow myself to be fooled anymore, I had to be one step ahead. No alcohol, in fact I wouldn't accept a drink from anyone. I was offered a room for free, so I took it. I cannot describe the relief I felt when I discovered there were two others at his house, a couple - an Austrian lady and her Greek lover, who were hiding away there to pursue their love affair. I felt safe after the initial turning down of 'Danny's' advances. He was fine about it. He turned out to be quite kind, decent and understanding albeit a little disappointed that I didn't want to sleep with him. He was a prison guard and worked day shifts, so I didn't see him much. My room was sparse but clean, there were fresh white sheets on the bed, a chest of drawers and a bedside table. It was on the first night that Danny propositioned me. I'd gone to bed, he knocked on the door and spoke a few Greek words that I didn't understand so I handed him my translation book which I kept with me at all times and he fumbled through it finding the words he was looking for and strung together a sentence that was something like "you, me, sex?" to which my answer was just the one word "no". I slept well that night. I was awoken by a cockerel which I found quite comforting, the sun was rising and burning through the early September mist. The house was silent, and I crept as quietly as I could to find the bathroom which was tucked away behind the kitchen. I noticed that somebody had been up already and left a note on the fridge. It was for me written in basic English telling me to eat breakfast.

On the table was a bowl of olives, a loaf of bread and a warm pot of coffee. It was perfect.

The loved-up couple soon appeared, and we sat together flicking through our phrase books, communicating as best that we could. English being the common language, it was a struggle, so we reverted to using signs. Later the couple showed me around the island. It had beautiful, pebbled bays, deserted, the water was aqua marine, the clearest I'd ever seen. In the lively market town was a mini carnival happening. From what I could see, there were very few tourists. I could really feel the Greek vibe, the ancient culture that lies hidden in many of the other islands or is so commercialised that it loses its appeal. Leros kept its charm and beauty although there was the underlying sadness and chaos within the prison walls.

I was made to feel very welcome; nobody knew anything about me but accepted me and kept me safe and fed. Leros had turned out to be the perfect place for laying low and passing the time until the money from Evan arrived at the bank in Athens.

A few days later I boarded the boat to Piraeus. I couldn't afford the ticket but it was a night crossing so I slipped through the queueing passengers and found a quiet spot to hide out. I was worried I'd get thrown off again so wrapped myself up with layers of dark clothes, put my head on my rucksack and was left alone, curled up and unspotted for the 12 hour crossing to the mainland. The money was in my account by the time I arrived in Athens. I should have felt some kind of joy and relief, but I felt nothing except for anxiety for what I was returning to. Nevertheless, I bought my ticket and flew back to England the very next day.

When I returned, I was reunited with Evan. I had nowhere else to go really and he had paid for my flight. I owed it to him.

We hadn't split up, but I had changed. I could see things clearer, I hadn't missed him at all.

I knocked on the door of his friend's house, his 'partner in crime' Harry. Evan answered the door, his eyes had that familiar look about them, black and piercing, magnetised and accentuated by the lense's in his national health spectacles. I'd learned to recognise and mentally prepare myself for that look but this time was different. I felt real fear, gut wrenching fear for what I knew was about to happen and I was too mentally exhausted to cope with it. The greeting which consisted of a tight-lipped kiss and "how was your journey?" was brief. Within minutes the violence started, following accusations and jealous drug induced paranoia. I expelled the pain and trauma of his actions out of both ends of my body simultaneously. It was the most un-dignifying experience. I tried to clean myself up before running out the door to the nearest phone box where I finally, without hesitation, called my dad. I told him everything, he could hear the desperation in my voice, and I could hear the relief in his. I admitted to what he already knew about the last two years of abuse I'd been through, and I promised to leave that man forever. Once I had made that decision, I felt lighter. I could see a future; I had no idea what it looked like, but it was a clear road ahead and I was going forward.

⸻◈⸻

Chapter 3

Light above the sea

In the cold water I find it hard to breathe

If I take one more step, I know I'm in too deep. The sand will slip between my toes,

the ice in the water chilling my bones and I'll sink in, deeper and deeper.

Up above in the shimmering light,

I see you and I'm trying to get back to you,

I can swim against the current, find a way out,

I know I can be saved, I have no doubt,

Just throw me a rope and pull me in the right direction.

It's a long way down but I can see light above the sea

It's a long way down and I'm heading for the light above me

It's a long way down, I can see you reaching out for me

It's a long way down and I'm heading for the light above me.

I can live through ripples, move with the tide,

I can jump over waves that crash in my life but I need a rock to cling to when I feel I'm sinking.

I can swim against the current find a way out, I know I can be saved, have no doubt

Just throw me a rope and pull me in the right direction.

It's a long way down and I can see light above the sea

It's a long way down and I'm heading for the light above me

It's a long way down I can see you reaching out for me

It's a long way down and I'm heading for the light above me.

Apart from the fact that I was now safe and away from my abuser, I was emotionally damaged, I realised that. I had never felt so broken and detached from myself and from the world around me. I didn't know how to reconnect. I was numb. I couldn't see any beauty in the world, just darkness and pain. I didn't listen to music and my guitar just collected dust. To become numb is nature's way of protecting yourself against emotional pain, to learn to feel again is a big risk so you must find a safe environment and even then, the process is slow.

Looking back on those days and my years of recovery is a good reminder of how important it is to be kind to yourself; your mental health is as important as your physical health. I've learned to nurture my own needs to help other people with theirs and one of the most important ways is to stay connected to who you are and to love yourself no matter what. You can never be anyone else so you must make the most of who you are and what you can contribute to the world and those around you. To enjoy all that life can give you, first you must enjoy your own company and understand and realise what your needs are and who you are.

A quote I found in a book I read recently, one of many of Mary's that I hope she doesn't mind me using but it resonated with me, so I would like to share it...

'The deeply personal is what connects us to the universal, the severing of the connection with the universal because of trauma and addiction is life threatening; re-joining it is a fundamental component of survival'......Mary Gauthier. ('Saved by a song')

It had taken years to get myself to this dark place, beyond fear, beyond care, a place of self-loathing and detachment, I knew things wouldn't be easy. I was one of the fortunate ones though, who was loved by my family when I was growing up and developing. I was given that grounding and was healthy and balanced, with enough self-worth to get through most things in life. Unfortunately, though when my mother died, I lost sight of that. My Dad was rebuilding his life and I didn't know how to move on with mine. It could take years to find myself and to love the world again. I couldn't do it by myself. I was in danger of self-destruction through alcohol and drugs. I was sinking into a sea of darkness, and I had to find that hand that was reaching out to save me.

The Ship

Accepting help was hard, I felt like a failure and the last thing I wanted was to be a burden on anyone. Dad had no idea what to do with me. It was a difficult one, but we came up with solution, I would have done virtually anything just to be away from Henley and Evan. It wasn't convenient to stay at dad's, but I trusted the idea he came up with that I needed to get away and go somewhere safe where I was cared for. Dad decided to send me off to stay with my grandparents in Sweden, Mormor and Morfar.

Their house reminded me of mum, she would take us annually when we were children. There was a comforting scent that was always there, a mixture of pine, cardamom and dill weed. It always felt safe there. I inhaled deeply, remembering the scent. I needed to feel again, Sweden was the place to start feeling and connecting.

They also had a summer house in Smögen overlooking the sea. It had had a similar smell about it with the added overtones of boiled potatoes and Cray fish. There were balconies and window boxes cascading with geraniums. We would sit and watch the boats and the tourists walking up and down the board walk. One summer whilst having morning coffee on the balcony a ship sailed into the harbour. I remember feeling its presence before seeing it, similar to a very distant rumble of thunder just before a storm. Its wooden mast stood tall, seagulls flocked around it and there was a choir on board singing 'How great thou art.' Mum got quite emotional at the time.

I wrote a song about that experience called 'The ship'. It's on my album 'Book of life'. The song came to me whilst looking through some old photos. I was feeling nostalgic, and I wanted to turn that feeling into music and make something positive out of my melancholic thoughts. We recorded it in Garry's studio adding sounds of seagulls. One of the things I like about that song is that it's not just about the ship, it's a song about a song. 'How great thou art' - it also paints the image in my mind of Smögen which is a beautiful island off the west coast where many Scandinavians go to with their yachts.

Smögen.

'The ship'

I hear a sound, a distant song
I feel the vibes running through my bones
All around the harbour people stand and gaze
Their eyes wide open, their hearts filled with praise
Here from the rooftop the force is strong
The sound gets louder, people singing along
The sails appear like giant seagulls' wings
The ship approaches while the choir sings.
I see a ship sailing into the bay
All the beautiful people raise their arms and wave
Then sings my soul while the music plays
How great thou art
How great thou art
The seagulls fly all around the sails
The mast stands tall, but the sound prevails
The choir sings from deep within their hearts.
The orchestra plays how great thou art.

Dad spoke to Mormor and Morfar and they were delighted that I was coming to stay. It was very short notice and I'm sure they had a few sleepless nights about it, but they wanted to help. They booked me a one-way ticket by boat. We left for the port in good time, but dad got lost as he often did. His navigation skills were pretty poor, and he'd get himself into such a state. We were pulling up as they were closing the gates. Swearing and all guns blazing in the ticket office, my dad insisted they let me on the boat but the trembling man behind the counter declined. There was only the one ferry going that day to Sweden.

However, there was a boat going to Denmark, so dad suggested I took that instead and hitch hike from Helsingborg to Karlstad, Sweden. Yes, it was certainly do-able but not ideal, I was tired and too traumatised as it was. My survival instincts would have to kick in again, I would have to find that sense of adventure and just do it. So, I did. My adrenaline kicked in, I was excited, though a little apprehensive. I'd hoped I wouldn't have to put myself through anymore potentially dangerous uncertainties but silently I was buzzing inside.

The boat to Denmark left the port with me on it, sailing away from my troubles, off to new pastures. Dad really should have called my grandparents and informed them that I wouldn't be arriving in Gothenburg 26 hours later, but he must have forgotten. He knew I'd get there eventually and I kind of liked that he had faith in me and my survival strategies. I stood out on the deck until I could no longer see land. It was cold and windy, and I was getting damp and sticky by the salty molecules in the air. I wasn't particularly concerned about how I'd get to Sweden from Denmark even though I had very little money on me. I had always thought of the Scandinavians as being decent people. I was more concerned about how rough the sea was going to get and figured I'd go and sit in the bar while I was still feeling well enough, maybe try and make some useful connections.

I ordered a scotch on the rocks and pulled out a stool. Scotch was my go to comfort tipple, it made me feel calm and relaxed. Ironically it was Dad that introduced it to me. As a child I had the job of pouring him a measure as he sat in his reclining chair in the evenings. It was one of those bonding rituals. We had a few, like sitting in the cabin of his long base land rover on a Saturday morning pricing up jobs. He would buy us both a Terry's Turkish delight and share with me his thermos of coffee.

Beside me at the bar sat a man who had the same idea as me, the ice in the glass clinking as we nervously circled it around the golden liquid. I figured he wasn't much into stormy waters either. He looked pleasant and friendly without the predatory look of a lot of Greek men I'd met. The bartender was young, approachable and chatty. He spoke perfect English as opposed to the man on the stool who couldn't seem to speak a word other than hello. I had grown used to flitting between languages trying to understand the general subject of the conversation. Swedish and Danish were quite different though so there was a fair bit of confusion. After another scotch I plucked up the courage to ask the bartender if he could possibly ask around to find out if anyone was travelling to Sweden. He said he could radio signal the lorry drivers down below. It turned out that the chap next to me was actually Swedish and was heading straight there from the port. It seemed like the perfect solution.

There were some awkward situations like the fact that we couldn't speak the same language and when we arrived at the port in Denmark and drove off the boat we were ushered straight into customs to be searched. It took the police and their dogs a good couple of hours to investigate the car as well as our luggage and us. I was wondering a little anxiously what I'd got myself into as was he about me which I had later discovered. It turned out that his car had been flagged up because he had taken that return trip in one weekend which is quite unusual. He'd been picking up some parts from England for his car and stood out as a potential drug smuggler.

We drove for a while in slightly uncomfortable silence until we got to the Oresund bridge. Crossing over to Sweden was a relief which I thanked him kindly for and I was happy to say goodbye and be on my way but he continued to drive on to an industrial estate. I was a bit concerned and confused but his expression and body language was calming and warm and I trusted he would do the right thing by me, he reminded me of Morfar, my Swedish grandfather. His whole demeanour was very honest and gracious. He pulled up beside a building, it looked like a factory, and we went inside. I couldn't help but wonder if this was another one of my naive moments, but he picked up the telephone and called his wife. They spoke briefly and then he handed the phone to me. The lady spoke perfect English and explained that I was to stay the night in the office upstairs on my own and in the morning at 9 her husband would be back, and he would take me to Malmö train station where I would board a train to Karlstad. I felt uneasy, it was almost too good to be true. In the office was a coffee making machine and a pull-out futon style bed. He handed me sheets and a blanket, set an alarm clock for 8 am and left. In the morning, as promised he arrived laden with home baked Swedish cinnamon bread, he took me to the train station, bought me a ticket to Karlstad and waved good bye as I boarded. I couldn't remember the last time I felt so blessed. That man's name was Johnny, I took his phone number so I could arrange to pay him back the train fare. I think I was meant to miss that boat to Sweden because that selfless gesture had restored my faith in humanity. I eventually turned up at my Grandparents house albeit a day late. They'd been so worried about me that they had Sweden praying for my safe arrival on their national Christian radio show.

Mormor and Morfar.

I spent about 6 months with Mormor and Morfar which was, in hind sight, exactly what I needed. They nurtured me, cleared up my overdraft that had built up whilst looking after mum and they fed me good healthy food. I joined a school, predominantly for refugees to learn Swedish and in doing so I met some great, interesting people from war torn countries. One of the friends I made was from Iraq, he was a poet and his words shocked me. I realised then how fortunate I was. I started to repair my damaged soul and learned to value myself and my life a bit more, most importantly I learned how to grieve. It wasn't easy as I was encouraged to face the trauma all over again which I had tried to bury. Mormor knew what she was doing, she had faced a lot of trauma in her life which led her to do work for the church and she then progressed to become a grief counsellor. More importantly though, she had lost a daughter, so our pain was shared. It was good to see mum's sister, Barbro; the similarities between her and Mum were quite surreal, their voices and expressions were uncannily the same and there were moments when it felt like mum was there.

For the first couple of months, I barely picked up the guitar. I was going through a process, trying to learn how to like myself, trying to accept the things that had happened without all the self-blame. It was tough. I joined a gym and swam every day. I put on a healthy amount of weight, started taking care of myself and allowing my Grandparents to look after me for a while. Evan used to tell me that I was fat and criticise me every time I finished the food on my plate. I was actually becoming too thin. My Grandparents noticed and made sure I ate three meals a day. They were vegan, and they fed me raw vegetables, nuts, beans and pulses. It was the healthy break I needed for my body and mind.

School was good for me. We were quite a mixed bunch there. We communicated mainly in Swedish as that was the language, we were all trying to learn but often we would switch to English as it was the most commonly known language amongst us. We were of all ages, and each had our own very different stories. There were a couple of mothers from Somalia, young men from Iran and Iraq, an English man who'd married a Swedish woman, and Ning from Thailand who had married a Swedish man. Ning and I became best friends. She joined me every day for swimming, and we spent evenings together at her house. She had 2 young children of her own when she married Rune, he took good care of them all. They lived a couple of streets away from me and I would walk down after supper, and we would spend the evening drinking whiskey and chatting. Nothing went unnoticed with my grandparents, and I think they were concerned about my escaping to Ning's as being a negative thing, but she was my saviour, I couldn't have endured 6 months in Sweden without her. Although my mother was Swedish, I felt like an outsider. I had no particular Swedish friends, they were so hard to get to know and my cousins were so much younger than me. I spent time in bars and cafes on my own and would try to make conversation with people but they were a bit sceptical of me and unresponsive. Mum always said to me that Swedes were naturally unfriendly towards strangers but once introduced through a mutual friend they will be friends for life. She was quite astounded when she first arrived in England as an au-pair and saw how people would say "morning" or "afternoon" to each other whilst walking the dog or strolling through the town even though they were completely unknown to one another. Whilst visiting Sweden one day she tried it out and got many strange looks but mostly ignored. She continued never the less and eventually people started to respond in a more positive way. I was shyer and more reserved than mum though and used the more ambiguous "have you got a light?" approach which of course was always taken literally. It was one extreme to the other coming from Greece and going to Sweden but in hind sight being a bit of a loner was good for me. It gave me the chance to think, observe, to look within myself and to connect again to the world around me. It's the little things in life that can easily go unseen and appreciated.

I was Christmas shopping one day and looking for a present for my little brother. I stopped at a market stall on the high street in Karlstad that was selling handmade Egyptian artefacts and jewellery and I was trying to choose an appropriate pendant for a teenage lad. It was one of those moments where I felt an incredible aura around the couple behind the stall. It was a blistering cold day but their warmth and light shone through them and I ended up telling them a bit about my sorry situation. Continuing to search through the beautiful pieces and trying to choose the right gift I found the one that I knew he would like; it was masculine enough and attached to a leather thong. The chap on the stall wrapped it up in tissue and popped it in a tiny velvet pouch and then said to me, "What do you think your brother would choose for you?" I pointed at another pendant and said, "Probably that one." The chap then wrapped the second pendant in tissue, popped it into another tiny velvet pouch and said, "This is for you from your brother." He wouldn't let me pay for either pendants and wished me a happy Christmas as I went on my way. I think that was my first step in accepting human kindness from a stranger without being cynical and it felt good.

I had no plan at all of what I wanted to do with my life or where I was going but I knew that I couldn't stay in Sweden forever.

Skiing with my friend Ning in Sweden,

Not much had changed back in England over the months. Evan was on a mad hunt for me, he failed to understand or accept why I'd left him. He was angry with everyone and tried getting information from my friends and family as to where I was. No one would tell him, my friends protected my wish to lie low. Just by chance though Evan found Vicky's phone book. The address and number were in it. He called me at my Grandparents', my safe place where I was recovering. His voice sounded desperate, he threatened to kill himself if I didn't go back to him. He went from being profusely apologetic to manically aggressive. I hung up the phone feeling an overwhelming mixture of guilt and fear. The anxiety was back, my stomach was in knots, and I felt like I would never be free of him. My safe place and privacy had been invaded.

Having experienced abuse and torment and coming out the other side of it made me more understanding towards other people in similar situations. It took a lot of time and self-belief to rid that feeling of being ugly and useless. Consistent, unconditional love will help to strengthen the soul but to find your own self-respect and worth when it has been repeatedly knocked out of you mentally and physically takes a long time. When I wrote the song 'Little man' years later, I knew I had faced those demons square on and beat them. In fact, I had become a stronger person.

I left Sweden in the middle of winter. I was looking better and feeling strong enough to face the world again. Morfar took me to the train station in Karlstad which would arrive in Gothenburg where a cousin of my mother's would meet me and drive me to the docks. I had met him before on family occasions at a lake house we used to go to for weekend gatherings. He was a dark haired, striking looking man with blue eyes, called Stora, meaning 'strong'. I knew I'd recognise him when I saw him.

In my childhood we went to Sweden most summers. We either drove through France, Belgium, Holland and Germany and caught a ferry from Denmark to Sweden or we would catch the overnight crossing from Harwich to Gothenburg. I preferred the drive. It took a few days, but we had fun along the way. Mum had her Neil Diamond collection playing and we kids would sprawl across the back of the yellow and black jeep padded with pillows and duvets. Mum had another cousin who lived in a castle in Germany. We would spend a couple of days there, living like royals and be spoilt rotten. They would hoist the Swedish and English flag up on our arrival.

The crossing from Harwich to Gothenburg took about 24 hours and the sea got very rough at times, especially the North Sea and I would get quite sick. I struggled a bit even as a young adult so before heading off back to England my grandmother who was aware of this gave me a special sea sickness remedy in the form of a plaster that sticks behind the ear and is slowly released through the skin into the blood stream. She recommended that I put it on before boarding the train to Gothenburg. It being a two-and-a half hour journey on the train the medicine would be working by the time I boarded the boat. It seemed like a great idea. I stepped onto the train with my guitar and a small case, waving Mormor and Morfar goodbye and feeling a sense of freedom mixed with fear and excitement. I was on my own again. My future was very uncertain, but I was going to hide out in London for a while.

Emotionally and mentally, I was in a much better place.

20 minutes into the journey I started to feel very odd. I can't really describe it except that my mouth going very dry and I think I was hallucinating. I looked around at all the other passengers as they read their books or papers so I fumbled about in my bag and decided on maybe having the snack that

Mormor had packed for me. I pulled out a biscuit and bit into it. It was tasteless and crumbled like dry cement in my mouth so I started to spit and reached out for what I thought was a cup of coffee in front of me but I'd just imagined it, so felt a little silly. I panicked a bit, confused, frustrated and desperately thirsty while eyes were staring at me from all directions. It seemed like a really long journey and my lips were sticking to my teeth. I don't think I had made the link at this point that I was having a reaction to the plaster behind my ear. My cognitive functioning was too impaired to do anything about it but the relief I felt when the train stopped, and everyone was getting off was immense. I needed coffee, water, anything. As I went to disembark, my legs felt leaden and my small case might as well have been filled with concrete. I was being pulled further and further towards the ground. Searching for the exit I took a step down on to the platform, dropping my guitar and case to the ground. The next moment I was lying there on my back looking up at people while they were looking down at me with concerned, sorry looking expressions but too hurried to help. I tried to shout, sounds came out of my mouth, but they were incomprehensible. I couldn't move. I have no idea how long I lay there. Thankfully a man appeared and helped me up, he had broad shoulders and his strong arms lifted me with ease. From the ground he looked like a giant. It was Stora, mum's cousin. It had been a few years since I'd seen him and he'd aged a bit, but I didn't forget that face, his blue eyes and dark brown hair. He looked concerned but it was the same look that I was getting from everyone else that had stepped over or around me, it was pity. I'm sure he'd heard through the family grapevine about my problems and failures. He pulled me up and led me, staggering towards the car park, supporting all my weight with his one arm whilst I tried to string a sentence together. He asked me what I'd taken, or had I been drinking but the best I could do as my words were coming out all jumbled was point to my ear. Having bundled me into the car he drove speedily back to his house to get advice from his wife before driving me to the docks. They laid me down on the sofa and called a doctor. I couldn't understand the conversation, but I felt reassured by the tone of her voice on the phone. I wasn't so much scared as embarrassed. They helped me up and into the bathroom where they removed the plaster and with instructions from the doctor, they thoroughly washed the area behind my ear, gave me water which I swigged back, then bundled me back into the car and drove me to the docks to catch my boat. When I arrived at the port I was taken to the medical bay and was helped aboard by a medic who took me to my cabin. I must have slept for several hours but when I awoke, I was still confused and wobbly on my feet. I needed to find somewhere to get some drinking water and found a bar. It looked like night time but I couldn't really tell. At least I could feel my legs again. However, when I asked the bartender for a glass of water my words came out as something entirely different! By the time the boat arrived in the UK I felt normal, but I knew I would never repeat that journey.

Chapter 4

Silence of the night.

One thing in my life that I have always struggled with is sleeping, whether I'm anxious or excited or just trying too hard, I can't switch off the thoughts. When everything around me is silent the thoughts are louder; when there is noise around me, my head is a jumbled up mess. I wrote this song one night whilst remembering a time in Greece where my friend and I did a séance. As an insomniac it was probably the worst thing I could have done because I inadvertently invited a whole party of voices into my head, and it took a lot of time and work to get rid of them. Lyrically the song is simple, I wanted to put the emphasis on the sounds rather than the words, like ahhhhh's which sound like screams. Here is the song, and the story follows.

'Silence of the night'

Sounds in the night, they echo through my mind, conversations, questions to myself.

Wish I could turn it down, try to erase the sound, so I can hear the silence, oh let me feel the silence. Give me the silence of the night.

My body's cold my bed is warm, very soon the night will turn to dawn.

The sound is getting louder, my heart is beating faster, and I am shouting to myself.

Oh, let me hear the silence, let me feel the silence, give me the silence of the night.

Hiding out in London for a while I got a job working as a door-to-door sales person. I couldn't risk going back to Henley and bumping into Evan. I heard rumours that he tried to get to Sweden on a freight boat but only got as far as Germany. I had been gone six months and he was still frantically looking for me. I was staying with Ralph, a chap in a band, I met in Sweden whilst they were on tour. He invited me to stay and rented me their spare room. It was my sanctuary for a while, and it gave me time to reflect and decide what to do next. My Dad had given me a diamond encrusted ring which had belonged to my mother, she had inherited it from her grandmother. I had permission to sell it if I needed to. On Portobello Road in London there are a row of antique shops; some of them specialise in jewellery. I had a few quotes from various dealers and settled on £400. It was worth a lot more, but I wanted to get away. It was a cold miserable February, the room I was renting was basic with no heating and my job was depressing. I was struggling to make money with the pyramid sales company. London was a lonely place to live, I had no social life so on the odd occasion I would get the train to Shiplake and meet my friends at the Baskerville Arms for drinks and then jump on the last train back home. The journey was about an hour long both ways including the tube but worth it for a bit of familiarity. It was one of those nights at the Baskerville where I met Australian Jane. She was staying with her cousins James, with the white Rover, and his brother Steve. Jane and I hit it off straight away and we planned our trip. I had the cash from the ring and Jane had savings enough to do one last stint in Europe before returning overseas. We arranged to meet the next day in London and very spontaneously booked to tickets to Rhodes. The following day we were on our way.

There were definitely things I wanted to settle and face up to in Rhodes, people I considered confronting and a few that I never got the chance to say goodbye to. I felt strong enough to do that but the fact that I knew a bit of the language and was familiar with the island drew me back there. I was more aware and less naive, I felt I could face my demons of the earlier events and best of all, I was going with Jane, my Australian travel partner. Jane was a singer, she performed at weddings and other events as a soloist. She had a very pure, well-trained voice and grasped the skill of harmonising. She was tall, blonde and slim, with fine features and a great personality. It was an absolute joy to sing with her. We discovered how much we had in common within a few days. We flew to Athens and spent a bit of time there before catching the boat to Rhodes. As soon as we arrived, we hired a cottage and practised our set daily until we were ready to go out and busk.

I realised how hardened and fearless I'd become over the last few years which for me highlighted Jane's fragility. She had emotions that I'd forgotten existed. She would question my decisions and motives and my reply would be, "Well what's the worst thing that could happen?" meaning I feared nothing not even death. Jane had a good supportive family that loved her. I didn't feel particularly loved by anyone really except for my Grandparents but I could only think that I was nothing but a burden on them. They helped me out so much, but I felt that they thought they owed it to me as Mum had died and my dad had left and was getting on with his new life. I questioned whether he had palmed me off sending me to Sweden. When you feel like that you stop caring about yourself so that kind of made me feel free. For the first time ever, I felt detached from the misery that I carried around. There was no black hole, there was no wall, there was a long road ahead. I remember recognising that a cloud had lifted, my stomach was no longer in knots, I could sleep better. That grip of anxiety had loosened, I was not being dragged back into that dark place every morning. Instead I could see the world around me, smell the essence of life and taste the sweetness of the day ahead.

The cottage was basic, tiled floor, white walls, not much furniture just a double bed and a small table in the kitchen. It was February, the nights were very cold, and we had no heating, but we wrapped up warm, sat in the kitchen with a bottle of Ouzo and learnt songs. At night we had to share the one double bed and blanket and very soon we became great friends. We were like kindred spirits with our love for music and adventure.

The cottage on Rhodes.

Between the two of us we paid for a month's rent up front which didn't leave much for food, but I was sure we would get work and make money busking.

The days were sunny and quite warm, but it was too early in the year for tourists. The hotels and some of the tavernas were in mid construction, preparing for the holiday season. The first job we found was cleaning the rooms in a hotel that had been left from the previous season. Beds unmade and used bathrooms still dirty.

We worked hard for little money. The Greek Drachma was very weak, so it worked out about £3 an hour. Everything was cheap there though. Jane and I stood out as we were both young and blonde. I carried my guitar on my back. We attracted attention from men and women. People were inquisitive. It was too early in the year for many tourists, but we walked around in shorts and t-shirts hardened by the English winter whilst the Greeks were still in full winter attire.

Everywhere we went people would shout out to us to play them a tune. Sometimes we did, we sang for food, played a song to the Pitta giros man outside his van for pickings of meat. We played in restaurants for a plate of spaghetti Bolognese. We busked barefoot in the old town where the artists and the hippies were setting up for the summer to sell their handmade jewellery and artwork.

It was an exciting time for traders, everyday it got a bit warmer and a little busier. They would stand outside their shops and bars ushering people in. Restaurants were shoving menus in passers' hands. Jane and I were urged into a bar, it was quiet inside, just a couple of Greeks. They gave us free drinks and peanuts. Before we left, the bar owner asked us to come back for two hours every evening at happy hour to just sit at the bar and drink for free. It sounded too good to be true, he even paid us. The bar started getting busy, people were buying us champagne. The peanut bowl was regularly topped up and plates of olives and antipasti kept coming.

We met a couple of nice lads, amongst the bunch of opportunists. George and Pandesis, they were young, geeky looking, spoke good English. They told us that what we were doing was wrong and that people were talking about us in a disrespectful way. These boys became our friends, they rode superbikes without crash helmets and rode us into town sometimes. They were enjoying the freedom of their final summer before doing a year's service in the army. Respecting what those lads recommended we gave up sitting in the bar like mannequins and got morning jobs instead, cleaning mainly. The rest of the time we explored the island, practised music and had fun.

Life was good. By April it was getting warm, and we had great tans. Both fed up with cleaning, we tried to make enough money busking all day instead. We sounded good and were getting booked to do gigs.

The unfortunate time came when we had to move out of the cottage. Stupidly we agreed to host an all-night séance, but it went very wrong. It was the first time we ever experienced anything like it. It was quite surreal and very scary. We met some people that did it regularly and initially we thought it would be just a bit of fun, but it left us both shaken up and we knew we had to get away from everything that reminded us of that night. The table in the kitchen still had the markings on and there was a ring of broken glass around it. What was once our temporary home now felt like it was possessed.

With our bags packed and guitar on back we headed for the port and caught a boat to Kos. We both really regretted what we had done. Interfering with the supernatural. It wasn't something we could easily shake off. Wherever we went that night came with us. I didn't want to believe, and I didn't understand even what it was that I didn't want to believe in after all, isn't it just a load of nonsense? So why was I so disturbed and why couldn't I sleep at night? My thoughts terrified me. I felt like I was being watched and there were spirits inside my head listening to my thoughts. My dreams were invaded, I woke up shaking, shivering in my bed. Was I possessed? I had to explore that possibility. I needed to turn off the voices and the noise in my head so I could feel, hear and drift off into the silence of the night but there was no silence or calm just noise.

Kos was in full swing, tourists everywhere, rows of clubs, young groups of Swedes and Germans, stags, hens, British tattooed lads and lasses.

Having secured a week's cheap accommodation on the island we went job hunting. Jane and I very quickly found work in a popular bar on the main drag serving drinks to tables. The hours were long, the money was poor, and our boss was a chauvinist. I didn't appreciate the way punters would grab and grope us. One night I had my skirt lifted by a group of lads for everyone to see and I was so humiliated and embarrassed. The next night I turned up in jeans and was told to leave so I did and never went back.

We stayed a few weeks, never really ventured off to other parts of the island but where we were, near the port, was soulless. Kind of like a pop-up town, probably a ghost town in the winter months. The long stretch of beach was crowded with oil drenched bodies, obsessively tanning themselves for their night out in the clubs. The place recked of sex, parties, fights and bad drunken behaviour. It wasn't for us, so we had to reconsider and plan our next step.

Going back to Rhodes was like going home. We weren't going to escape the mentality of the Greek men; they weren't all bad, a lot of them just lacked respect for western women. They were very charming in their own way and yes, we were exploited but it was our choice whether to live with it or not. Rhodes had something special about it. The old town, within the castle wall was very historical and filled with character, cobbled streets, little shops and tavernas, lots of backpackers from all over the world. We were comfortable going back and it felt right but not to the same place, the island was big enough to settle somewhere new.

Hidden away down one of the back streets was a hostel called 'Pythagoras'; it was run by an elderly man. It was the cheapest place to stay. Beds were crammed into dormitories. It was filthy, the showers were cold, and it was hard to get any sleep there, but it was cheap, and we met some great people from all over the world, musicians too. There were jam sessions every night, a bar with reasonable beer and a never-ending supply of popcorn. Everyone moaned about the place as it was so run down and a complete health and safety hazard, but it was too easy to stay and in a great spot to stagger home to late at night or early morning.

Jane and I decided not to bother looking for work, we were tired of being used. We didn't have work permits so employers got away with paying us pittance and it was soul destroying. Instead, we found our little spot where the artists sit and paint and the travellers sell their ware, from jewellery, leather pouches, to hand woven rugs. A few hours of singing would cover our costs.

I was asked out for a drink one night by a young Greek man. Normally I would have declined but he was nice looking in a not too obvious way, well dressed, tall and dark. He had kind eyes and was very respectful and polite. I made the effort to dress nicely, and he picked me up from the hostel. We went for dinner, followed by dancing. The conversation we had was intelligent and interesting and I really started to like him. It was a lovely evening and he walked me home. As we said goodbye, he kissed me on the cheek, and I ran into my dormitory feeling happy and excited. Sitting on the edge of my bed in the dark I heard a voice and looked up to see the outline of the man; he'd come back. Smiling and happy to see him, I stood up, thinking he wanted to say something or I'd maybe left something behind but instead he hit me hard on the side of my face and shouted something in Greek. I fell back onto my bed, pain searing through my jaw feeling completely and utterly confused. I never did find out what that was all about, but it threw me back into a state of unease. He must have been mentally ill or hurt in the past by an English girl and wanted to take his anger out on me. I think he planned it. For me though it was very upsetting. I'd let my guard down and taken a risk resulting in such strange and shocking consequences.

Since the séance I was still experiencing night terrors and we both felt that heavy dark cloud over us from that unforgettable night in the cottage. I needed help. I had to speak to someone that might understand what we were going through so we tried the church and spoke to a priest, we explained what had happened. Thankfully he took it very seriously and blessed us with holy water. The three of us prayed, he said that the bad spirits had left and his final words to us were 'good is stronger than evil'. We both felt immediate relief, lighter and more positive. I stopped fighting the conversations in my head, remembering those last words the priest said and later the bad thoughts subsided, the nights got easier, and the days became more fruitful.

We got by for a while, the tourists were generous, we afforded the rent, food and beer. Everything was going well until Jane got a bad cold and completely lost her voice. Busking gives you the freedom to be as flexible as you want but unless you make enough money to put some aside there are always times when you come unstuck, and this was one of them. I didn't feel I could do it on my own, my voice wasn't loud enough to cut through the hustle and bustle of a busy holiday island, so we had to find a job until Jane's voice returned.

Staying in the hostel was a good way of getting information about available work. Some of it was quite well paid too but you had to be up before dawn to get it. Our drinking had become quite a habit with the new friends we made, socialising till the early hours. So some mornings we would stagger from a beach party somewhere to the dry docks where they were recruiting on a first come first serve basis. I don't know how we did it but our job was to sand all the barnacles and tube worms off the hull of the boats. Barnacles secrete this sticky liquid glue type substance that hardens like cement. The work was exhausting but the money was reasonable.

Our lifestyle started to take its toll on our health. Jane's cold developed into a full-blown chest infection. She started feeling depressed. Previously to taking off on her European travel tour, Jane had suffered from depression. I was worried about her. It was time to get away, we'd slipped into a routine where we were burning the candle at both ends. The novelty was wearing off anyway and some of the friends we made in the hostel had moved on, so it was time for us to do so too.

I was quite shaken up by the incident with the Greek man that I dated and I wasn't in any hurry to get romantically involved but I had met a lad called Simon in the hostel. He was English, tall and broad. We started spending days and nights together. It had become quite a whirlwind romance. He stood out amongst the dark olive-skinned Greeks. His sun bleached, wind-swept hair fell gently over his mischievous eyes that sparkled when he laughed. He was a breath of fresh air. He had to leave amidst the bliss of getting to know each other to continue his around the world trip. It wasn't ideal falling for someone that was soon to be leaving and I was gutted when he kissed me goodbye and boarded the boat to Turkey. I watched as it sailed out into the horizon. We promised to keep in touch and meet up again one day.

Jane and I were both feeling a little lost and sad but kept a positive outlook. Looking at a map of mainland Greece we chose to head for the Peloponnese. There was enough money in the kitty from cleaning boats to sail to Piraeus and get a train to the southern tip of Greece. We had no idea what we were going to but excited about a new adventure. Boarding the train and finding a seat we dumped our heavy ruck sacks down beside us and headed off to new pastures. We prepared for a long journey, so we had no food or water. Not long into the journey but just enough time to doze off to sleep, the ticket lady appeared, tapped Jane on the shoulder and asked to see our tickets. Typically, there was an error, whether it was our mistake or the ticket office I don't know but our tickets were not bound for the Peloponnese, so we were told very bluntly that we had to get off at the next stop. Jane argued with the lady, it got quite heated so to our horror the ticket collector pulled the emergency chain to stop the train and threw us off right in the middle of nowhere. We were surrounded by wheat fields, not a road in sight; it was red hot and very dry. We had no provisions and no idea which way to walk. I can't remember feeling half as bad as Jane felt but I remember worrying about her. Jane often got annoyed with my care free attitude; even if I had been scared, I would not have wanted to show it.

Well things were very different in the early 90's. The mobile phone wasn't long out, and it was only really used by business people but we used phone boxes and wrote letters. We were stranded and things could have got bad, but we took a chance in one direction and eventually came to a road. Jane was a little reluctant to hitchhike but we had no choice. It wasn't long before a van pulled up. The chap was going to Korinthos, which at least was the right direction to where we wanted to go. He opened the back doors of the van which held a large tray of water with fish floating about in it; not ideal but we squatted in there, relieved to be back on the road. The chap was delivering to an island hopper boat that did tours on the Korinthian waters. When we arrived, we thought we'd ask if there was any work going on board. The captain showed us around and put us to the test by asking us to clean the staff bathroom and toilets. They were filthy, and we got them spotlessly shiny. He then tested our bar skills. He seemed happy and asked us if we could start immediately. It would involve living on board. I was ecstatic. Jane wasn't too thrilled though. I'm not sure exactly what happened but she had a sudden change of heart and wanted to return home to Australia. She had her return ticket and just needed to get back to Athens. She was tired and I don't think she could cope with more of the unknown. The following day one of the deck hands gave her a lift to the nearest town and she caught the train to Athens. It was quite upsetting and so final. We'd been through so much together. I was now going to have to cope on my own.

It was sad to see Jane go the next morning, but I had to respect her decision. She needed to see her family, they were worried about her, she'd been away for a year, and it was time for her to return home. Now all alone, the only woman on the boat amongst Greeks, an Albanian and one Turkish man but I wasn't afraid!

Naturally the crew on the boat 'Hera' were all very friendly. The captain, Costas, was young, in his 30's, very charming, good-looking and seemed to have a good relationship with the rest of the crew. Deck hands, Vangelis and George, were a bit older than me, mid to late twenties. The Albanian man, Nikos, was the engineer. He didn't speak much English but smiled all the time and was kind. He and the Turkish man who was the chef and bar manager were the only two on board that showed me any kind of respect, they treated me as their equal. Over time, as I learned more about the on-board politics I came to realise and accept that it was us and them. We were the foreign workers.

Unfortunately, I had to share a cabin with Vangelis and George. I had the top bunk and kept myself to myself.

Over the weeks we became quite good mates and had a laugh, but they said things that were chauvinistic and inappropriate, behind my back. I learned basic Greek and ignored the disrespectful comments from them over the dinner table. The job was fun, we did 8 hour trips every day, island hopping. Picking tourists up from their hotels and dropping them back at the end of the day. At the weekends we would switch to another boat, a Turkish gulet called 'Sea dancer' and we would host night parties. The owner of the two boats, Dimitri, would come on board whilst in the docks for meetings and to count the takings. He was short, rounded, with slicked back hair, dripped in gold jewellery. He never really spoke to me just clicked his fingers for me to bring him coffee - Greek coffee, made in the traditional way. He kept my passport in the head office in Athens, that was normal procedure. In fact, a passport for them to own me, pay me pittance and keep me there for as long as they wanted. I was a good worker, I had fairly good people skills and was polite and well spoken. I knew I was being taken advantage of, I had no fight with any authorities as I was working illegally but I looked at the job as a worthy experience. I saw a lot of the islands, had plenty of time exploring when we weren't working and I even got to steer 'Sea dancer' for nine hours through the night, sailing home from a long trip whilst the crew slept. It was a simple matter of keeping the line on the dot as it was pre-navigated. I loved that night, the sea was unusually still and tranquil the whole way. It felt like it was just me and the ocean on this beautiful wooden vessel. I was congratulated when I got everyone home safely.

The Turkish chef, Feruke, was a good man, he looked out for me, he was a little too protective at times, but I needed that. He regularly read my coffee cup after watching me endure the strong black bitter liquid. The sediment would sit at the bottom of the small china cup, and he would empty it on to the saucer after I'd finished drinking it. The cup and saucer symbolised past and future. He studied the shapes that had formed and warned me of things, dangers to be aware of. At the same time he liked to stick his nose in my business, quizzing and questioning me. I found it a little irritating at times.

Much to Feruke's disapproval, Nikos, the friendly Albanian offered me £1000 of his savings for me to marry him so he could get an English passport. I would have done it and even the chef's strong advice didn't stop the two of us venturing into Athens on our day off to explore the possibility. There were too many complications involved though so we didn't go ahead with it, but had it happened I would have gone to Africa after the summer season in Greece.

My next adventure took place when 'Hera' was closed for cleaning and renovations. The whole crew had to leave for a few days. Unlike me, they all had homes to go to or places to stay. I went for a three day walk. I left my guitar on board in my cabin and travelled light with my rucksack holding a change of clothes, a blanket, plus food and water. I stopped at a shop and picked up a map. I wanted to get to the end of the Peloponnese, which is the far tip of the peninsula. I realised it would take about 2 days to walk it or at least a day and night so I walked for about 5 hours sipping water and nibbling bread from my bag. The heat really got to me, I was sunburnt and exhausted, so I hitchhiked the rest of the way.

The first person to stop was a man in a pickup truck, good looking in a rugged way with dark shoulder length hair and a beard. His 2 young children sat in the front, they squeezed over so I could jump in, and they both stared up at me with their big brown eyes. I felt reassured and safe to begin with but 5 minutes down the road the man pulled over at a petrol station and urged the children to get out. Being naive, I assumed they were going to the toilet as they ran inside appearing to know where they were going. The man waved them goodbye, shouted a few words out to them and drove off leaving them behind. At that point I started feeling nervous. The man said little to me and couldn't speak much English. Looking at my map I was concerned when we drove off down a little road on the left, it led to a dirt track, I was frantically questioning the man, but he ignored me.

I shouted 'Asta' which is 'stop' in Greek, he continued, pretending not to understand me. I tried again and he voiced in very poor broken English 'we go make love' he was taking me to a hidden cove. The track was bumpy, he was driving slowly avoiding the dips and potholes. I shouted again 'Asta' to which he stopped the truck angrily. I opened the door and ran leaving my bag with everything in it behind. I was stranded but found my way back to the main road. It was hot, I had no water or money. It was too far to walk back to the boat; I would die of heat exhaustion. There was only one thing I could do. Hitch a lift down to the Peloponnese. Onwards and forwards.

I made it down there eventually and it was stunning, heaven on earth. I found water. I got talking to some travellers, they shared food with me, we chatted until the sun went down and they disappeared. I lay on the beach, it started to feel a bit chilly, but I had no clothes except for the shorts and t-shirt that I was wearing so I headed for the bar where I could sit for a while with a glass of tap water. Two elderly men started talking to me, they were a couple, lovers or brothers, I wasn't entirely sure, but they didn't seem at all predatory, more caring and concerned. I was feeling quite ill, possibly sun stroke and they asked me where I was staying. When I said I was sleeping on the beach they were shocked and insisted I go with them. I was in no fit state to argue as I was feeling very nauseous. They bought me a whiskey from the small taverna, and I started to become drowsy, and my head was thumping. Strangely I wasn't scared, I went with them to their home in the forest close by. They made me up a bed, poured me tea and offered me a smoke of home-grown marijuana. The bed was in the kitchen, so I lay down and slept whilst they rattled around, quietly whispering and drying up crockery. I remember waking up and them sitting next to me stroking my hair and mopping my forehead with a cool wet cloth. I dozed in and out of sleep until the morning, they didn't leave my side. When I awoke, they gave me breakfast and drove me back down to the beach. I felt stronger but wanted to get back to the boat. I hitched 2 rides, the first one was an old man in a faded red pick-up who 10 minutes into the journey decided to undo his trousers and display everything. I learned to be blunt and use the word 'Asta' with the emphasis in the right place. By the time I got the second lift, I was shaking very much with fear when I jumped into the lorry, but the driver gave me a lecture to never hitchhike in Greece again. He told me that he'd only stopped because he didn't want me getting raped or worse. I really appreciated his concern, but I didn't have any choice. When I got back to the boat 2 days early Feruke was sat there on the deck enjoying the peace and quiet. He had decided to stay on board. If only I'd known, I would have stayed too. Most of the repairs had already been done. We spent the next 2 days making cocktails and reading coffee cups. It was interesting what he read about mine and he was pretty much spot on.

The following week we had all settled back into our work routine. The rest of the crew were back after their mini breaks. We had daily trips until the end of the season and some night ones too; it was going to be a very busy couple of months, but I enjoyed it. There were times when the sea would get very rough, and I'd be handing out sick bags and pills to tourists and even taking bottles off the shelves behind the bar. It was chaos at times but only for about 20 minutes and afterwards the sea would be completely still and calm like a pond. The captain would warn us in advance before it got very rough. We were all too busy and running off adrenaline to feel sick. I was terrified but had to keep a professional head on. It wasn't until the panic was over that the crew, including the captain, could lean over the side of the boat and vomit.

One of my favourite trips, a month before the end of the season was on 'Sea dancer'. It was a moonlight serenade party for a large group of Russians. I was working with the boss's son, he was a little younger than me and autistic. He struggled behind the bar, but I was on form in my element, loving every moment. The music was great, everyone was dancing, such beautiful looking people, I didn't have time to stop and have a break but downed the odd shot of vodka to keep me going. I could have made loads of money on tips. They were coming in fast, but I just placed them in the till. I was feeling euphorically happy that night, money was the last thing on my mind. Eventually the evening ended. We were clearing up party mess until 2am. I was the only member out of our usual crew working that night, the others were on 'Hera' which was docked in the same harbour. I was going to be paid extra as a separate job and chuffed to have been asked. They knew I was a good worker, and the punters always liked me. The boss's son was very sweet and respectful, he ran around collecting glasses and wiping tables. Finally putting my feet up, relaxing and reflecting on the evening's events, I poured myself a scotch, looked out at the stars and lit a long-awaited cigarette. I felt so fortunate and felt that the boss would be really pleased with me. I was thinking how I could do this sort of thing happily all year round. Whilst sat out on deck chilling, breathing in the night air and listening to the sounds of the fenders gently knocking against the jetty, the captain, Costas, from the other boat appeared. He told me I was wanted back in the office on Hera. I was intrigued but initially unconcerned. When I boarded the boat, the crew were acting oddly, something was up. It was my first time in the office, and I was asked to sit down. The stern expression on the boss's face clearly told me something was wrong. It turned out that there was some money missing from the till where I'd been working. They had counted the takings and it didn't add up. He accused me of stealing. I obviously denied it and explained that I also put every penny of my tips in the till. I didn't have pockets on me or a bag, but he didn't believe me and said I would have to leave. I was gutted, I cried so hard. The captain was nice to me, but he was dubious, I could see it in his eyes. The rest of the crew were unsure. I couldn't stress my innocence enough. I wanted to jump into the sea and disappear.

I barely slept that night but appeared reluctantly after breakfast whilst they were clearing away the dishes. Feruke was all smiles and greeted me with coffee and baklava, he was always on my side and the first to tell me that the boss had made a mistake and had miscounted the takings which meant that I was all in the clear. My first response was relief, followed shortly by fury. I had cried all night, I was scared, angry and humiliated by the accusations and lay on my bunk tossing and turning, worrying about what I was going to do. I had been accused of a criminal offence and might have even been arrested.

Feruke recommended that I go on strike until I had an apology. It wasn't like me to be defiant, but I did want an explanation and some sort of recognition for my hard work just out of courtesy. Well, everything went back to normal, work as usual. I told the captain that I wanted to speak to the boss. Unfortunately, he was unavailable. I was told to forget about the incident. I didn't forget how I'd been treated and my love for the job had been tainted. It might have been a silly move but I sent a message through the captain to head office saying that I wanted my passport back so I could leave. My request had been ignored and after several subsequent messages I had to let it go and continue working another month until the end of the season. My final day on that boat was a mixture of emotions. My passport came back but I wasn't paid for the month that I didn't want to be there so I had not only worked for nothing, but I was also broke. I had to find a way to get back to England.

It was late September. Tourism was winding down. My best bet and only option, really, was Athens.

Saying goodbye to the crew was bitter sweet. I felt sad to leave in a way but confused and angry, how could they wave me off knowing I had nowhere to go and no money? I felt worthless. With a small bag of light clothes and my guitar in my hand I was off again on my way to nowhere in particular.

Another adventure.

The temperature had dropped a few degrees for which I was grateful, and I had a big bottle of water and snacks to get me through the next day or two. I walked for hours, leaving early in the morning and just before sunset I hitchhiked the rest of the way, arriving in Athens by the evening. What I desperately needed was a job. I found a hostel, it was pretty run down and dirty. I asked if I could clean for them in return for accommodation, but they said that the dorms were full. I phoned my brother, Patrick, from the desk in the hostel, they kindly allowed me that privilege as long as I kept it short. Patrick had no idea of the situation I was in and as soon as I mentioned borrowing money, he turned cold and declined. I don't blame him, I was a nuisance to everyone. I put the phone down and walked out into the city smog. Apparently, Patrick had called the number back having changed his mind, but I had gone.

I tried to be strong, hold my head up and not be a target for users and abusers. I stood out though as a lonesome traveller and constantly attracted the wrong attention. I ignored every remark, every whistle, every grope and just walked.

The Warrior

I met a man, warrior, he was holding a shield, escaping from what had become a dangerous battle field. I tried to help him lose his guard, I said I'm not the enemy, he just sighed, said life is hard and so it will always be. He marched off into the night, laden with his woes, clad in coat of armour from his head down to his toes. He was heading nowhere and nowhere he would go, so, I called, "hey warrior, it's time to take you home."

I said "come over here, come over here and talk to me my friend, you're not alone and not on your own, this is not the end, we all have our worries, we all have our fears, but time will mend broken lives and time will dry our tears, hey warrior."

I could see that he was fighting with the cross he had to bear, the enemy stood firmly but he lost the will to care.

Alone he marched and he embarked on a life of self-defeat, the world became his rival and the world he would retreat.

So, I said "take off your armour warrior, throw away your shield, discard all your weapons and talk to me."

I said "come over here come over here and talk to me my friend, you're not alone and not on your own, this is not the end. We all have our worries we all have our fears, but time will mend broken lives and time will dry our tears. hey warrior."

The warrior had generated a lot of interest amongst war veterans as we did a video to it which can be found on YouTube as well as our Facebook page and the video shows real WWI footage. In the literal sense it is about a war veteran that is struggling during the aftermath of battle. When I wrote the song, I used words metaphorically to describe a person, victim of their own personal battle who is trying to overcome their depression and anxiety, addictions, afflictions or whatever hardship they may be facing.

In my life and during my travels I've met the most incredibly strong people that have left a lasting impression on me. One of them was a Danish man who travelled to Greece in the 1970's on a one-way ticket and never made it back home. He lived as a vagrant in Athens. He was a dying man when I met him, literally on his last leg as the other was becoming gangrenous and there was no hope of medical treatment for him. So many people suffer within their internal wars, fighting some kind of persecution or struggling to pull themselves out of their troubled lives. PTSD comes in many forms and it can be such a silent suffering where very little is out there and people are reluctant to seek it, especially where shame and blame are concerned. We all have our battles and fears and although time is indeed a great healer we still have to live with the scars and the memories forever remain.

The way I saw the world changed that night in Athens and I changed too. I now regarded myself officially homeless. Not a traveller, certainly not a tourist but a homeless victim of circumstantial unfortunate events. I had fallen several times and still I kept falling, finally I had hit rock bottom. I spent the night with vagrants on a bench in Victoria Square, we begged around the open-air restaurants, I saw my reflection through the eyes of wealthy Greeks and it sickened me but I numbed my pain with the whiskey we afforded ourselves with our earnings. The hobos in the park appreciated having me there as I strummed my guitar around the tables. People took pity on me being a young female and destitute so they gave quite generously. Although I must have looked like an alcoholic or a drug addict, I was still relatively fit and healthy. I learned a lot about my new friends. They were all originally travellers, who like me got lost along the way. The kind Danish man who shared a corner of his blanket with me had gangrene in his foot. The smell was putrid. I didn't sleep that night, but I felt safe. These chaps showed me human kindness that I had forgotten existed.

Laced with gold

Through bustling cities and dirty old streets,
Deserted old villages, hills that are steep,
I head for the freeway, away from it all,
Look for the place with the trees that are tall

There's no turning back, there's nothing behind
I keep heading onwards,
I know I must find that place that is heaven and I have been told
At the end of the rainbow the sky is laced with gold.

I'll walk to the edge of the world
To the end of the rainbow until I am old, and I'll find the gold.

Galloping horses are passing me by
Fattened up birds are ready to fly
To a place in the south, a place where it's warm but the predators wait for the migrating swarm
I know it ain't easy
Life isn't fair
Some of us don't make it
Some of us don't care
But I keep heading onwards
Until I am old
At the end of the rainbow
The sky is laced with gold.
I'll walk to the edge of the world
To the end of the rainbow until I am old
And I'll find the gold.

My life had become a whole row of hurdles in which I usually managed to jump with all the enthusiasm I could muster only to fall on my face on the other side, but I kept jumping. If I saw a potential opportunity, I went for it. I liked to see the good in people, but it was wearing thin. I did believe one thing though. Eventually I would land on my feet.

In the morning I made tracks, through seeing myself the way others saw me with that sorry look in their eyes I knew I had to move on. If I didn't leave now, I would be hitting the bottle every night, it was a slippery slope, and I was sliding. There had to be a way out, an opportunity, I had to keep going. There was no plan, I was relying completely on the gods, on chance, luck, my angels, signs, anything to guide me to a solution. Mentally I was strong under the circumstances, but a wave of emotion came over me and my face became flooded with tears as I sat on a bench in a park. There were lots of tourists about with cameras around their necks. I doubled over and my body shook as I let go of some of my pain, for that short time I didn't care, I had to release that sadness and desperation. It felt good to cry but I had to stop before somebody spotted me. Wiping away my tears I sat up, some of the cloud and darkness within me had shifted. It was a beautiful day I could see it now but couldn't feel it. Happy people everywhere going about their day, learning, exploring, taking in the scenes, the history, the culture. I watched a group of young travellers. They stood out amongst the tourists, dishevelled, ungroomed but practical as they rattled along with their various kitchen utensils hanging from their backpacks. Looking far too over dressed in walking boots and anoraks tied around their waists. They spotted me, I felt silly like Billy Nomates, but I didn't care. I put my head down so they couldn't see my swollen eyes, but they continued to watch and started heading towards me. I wished they would go away, I was in no position to talk or give directions, I knew nothing about my surroundings or what the park was called or what the big white building was that everyone was taking photos of. I was nothing more than a vagrant trying to survive, wondering where and when my next meal would be and where I would lay my head that night.

Holding my guitar close to me and looking down towards the ground trying not to look how I felt conscious that, a hand reached out to tap me on my shoulder. I looked up to see three lads, the travellers. They stood looking down at me. They were a mismatched trio - one chap looked Oriental, the other a scruffy young red head and the third slightly older and tidier in appearance. It was obvious to me that they had set out individually and hooked up. They had seen that I was upset and asked if I was ok. I ended up telling them a bit about my ordeal and that I was stranded. They were off to Crete the next day to look for work. After a considerable amount of time swapping stories, they invited me to join them. They offered to lend me some money for the crossing and kindly put me up that night on the floor in their hostel. It was the perfect solution, the only solution; I felt blessed and so relieved, apart from anything else I had nothing to lose. My assumption was correct, they had all met travelling alone and had basically taken pity on me and asked me to join their pack. One of the chaps was Irish, another was Hungarian and then there was the Chinese lad who later gave me his lucky dollar, given to him by his uncle which I treasured for the next 30 years.

We arrived in Crete the next day. It was a relief to get away from the busy city and great to be by the sea. However we were in a resort called Malia and the summer season was still thriving, full of youngsters, it was well known as the party resort of the island.

We went foraging in an olive grove. I showered on the beach and tried my first sea anemone. I realised I hadn't eaten for three days so it tasted good. I felt safe again, so we parted ways. My saviours had helped me out big time and now I had to go it alone, find a job and somewhere safe and quiet to lay my head. I didn't forget those guys and told them I would pay them back the money they spent for my ticket once I'd started earning. It was a small enough resort to bump into them. I would find them in one of the many bars if I looked and asked around.

The sun was going down and I was alone again with not a penny to my name. I walked as far as I could away from the hustle and bustle up along the street towards the main freeway, away from the noise and far enough out from the bars and cafes. It was agonising watching people eating in the restaurants as I passed by and the smell of grilled chicken filled the air. I continued walking, away from the mouth-watering sights and smells.

Up ahead in the distance I spotted an old church on top of a hill and wondered what the view would be like from up there. I wondered what Malia would be like without tourism, just old decrepit houses, a deserted village of crumbling white washed stone. I made my way up a winding cobbled street. It was hot, I was sweating and had no water but kept going until I reached the church.

Strangely it felt like l was going to meet someone. Opening the heavy door, stepping inside was like I was arriving at a place where I had been invited, like someone was waiting for me and I was on time, appropriately dressed and welcome. I had nothing to offer, I looked shabby and worn, tired, hungry and falling apart at the seams but it didn't matter, I had been summoned and my present state was entirely acceptable. I strolled in, the cool temperature was such a welcome relief. There was a jug of water and paper cups in the entrance next to a flowing spring in the wall. I helped myself and tasted the sweetness of the minerals, I put my hands in the spring and splashed my face, washing away the salty sweat and dried tears from the previous day. I relished in the spirituality of the experience, walking in the shadows of millions of other people before me. It was quiet inside, no music just the imaginary sounds in my head of an angel choir. Flickering candles beckoned me and a very elderly lady in black was lighting one and placing it next to the others before kneeling and praying. I copied her but instead of praying to a holy god whom I had little belief in, I spoke to my mum, I asked for direction, signs and inner peace. I realised it was only me that could get myself out of the mess I was in, but I needed guidance, I needed someone to believe in me instead of pitying me. My Mother believed in me. I had lost faith in myself, I stumbled from one disaster to the next. Something had to change, the cycle had to be broken and reset. Placing the lit candle into the holder and staring into the flame I said my words, thanked the heavenly host for inviting me and walked out into the glorious sunshine.

The view was incredible. There was a hazy mist over the town, but the sea was visible with the outline of a ship on the horizon, the sky was laced with gold streaks. I was looking at the most stunning painting. Thankfully I could see beauty in the world again and I wanted to be part of it. I wanted to survive.

Walking back down the steep path towards the town of Malia I felt lighter. It was like I had left a big weight back up at the church. My rucksack felt less heavy on my shoulders, I even noticed a spring in my step, I tried a skip and smiled to myself. I think I had left my desperation behind and had replaced it with gratefulness. Today, I said to myself, was going to be a good day and it was.

One of the things I disliked about Greece was the multitude of fur coat shops. I didn't understand the need for them all, not only were they distasteful but completely unnecessary. The salesmen would stand outside and lure women in with their charm and false flattery, preying on the wealthy looking tourists, trying to ease money out of them; it was hard to watch. As I skipped down the road towards the party capital of Crete with my new enthusiasm towards life, I was very blatantly stopped by one of those pushy salesmen. Looking around me thinking he must be directing his pitch to someone else I realised it was in fact me he was aiming it at. Could he not see that I was no more than a homeless person that hadn't eaten for days? Instead of ignoring him and walking on, I stopped and chatted, who knows, he might just be a struggling employee working on a commission, desperate to be seen to be doing his job. I gave him the benefit of the doubt and allowed him to throw the whole pitch at me. It wasn't long before he realised that he was wasting his breath and I discovered that he was the owner of the shop. His next offer was to have me model his coats. He would pay me a small amount to walk around the shop in different coats and I would receive a commission for the sales. Had I been naiver I might have gone for it, I had nothing more to lose, but I declined. If I were to break the cycle of self-destruction, I had to see the trap. I later realised I had been given my first test and I passed. It would have been another disaster waiting to happen, another man to use his position of power over me. My layers of strength like emotional body armour were wearing thin and I had to protect myself. I had to use my experience and knowledge to keep myself safe, learn to trust my instincts and find some self-respect.

Holding my head high I continued down the street with my new look on life. I had the power to say no, I had options, and I knew what the bumpy roads looked like. I decided to take the next fork. I knew I had to find the confidence to do what others do. Having no fixed abode could be my downfall in trying to find a job but I had to at least try so I walked, and I talked, gave it everything I had and by the end of the day I was employed. I had 2 jobs, 1 in a cafe bar starting at 8am, the other in a night club starting at 9pm, there wouldn't be much time for anything else which I was more than happy about and the hours I had to sleep were minimal. The greatest thing about it was that I could eat at work and save all my money for a ticket home. I started my new job the very next morning at the Joker bar. It was ironic. My life had become more than a joke. The chef there had to leave in the midst of a busy season, and I came along just at the right time. The menu was all day breakfast which I could do easily. One of the waiters had a friend that was wild camping in the olive grove and said I could probably share his tent. I was given rough directions and after my shift in the night club I made my way up there. It was a two-man tent and I crawled inside next to him at about 4 am and slept for a few hours before getting up. The stranger beside me continued sleeping. I showered on the beach and made my way to the Joker bar for the 8am start. I never met my tent mate, but we slept beside each other every night until he left one day and took his tent with him.

Danser dans la nuit

*Dancer dans la nuit vous et moi, dancer dans la nuit
vers la lune dancer dans la nuit sous les etoiles*

*I'll give you my love if you will dance where nobody
can see, take my hand, spin me like a leaf that circles
softly to the ground.*

*Share with me your splendour and your charm,
Lovers in the dark bound as one,
Lost in all my senses I surrender to the moon.*

*I'll give you my love if you run your lips gently where
my hair falls against my cheek, hold me in your arms
while my knees go weak.*

*Take me to the valley beyond the stars, lead me to
the garden of wild desires, sway me like a willow,
blowing softly in the breeze.*

*I'll give you my love if you will dance and gaze into
my eyes like some romance in a never-ending story
or an unforgotten song.*

*Danser dans la nuit vous et moi, dancer dans la nuit
vers la lune dancer dans la nuit sous les etoiles.*

By 4 am the sun was soon to rise, and it was fairly warm, so I continued to return to that spot, I found an old blanket and slept under a tree. There was a pig tied to a chain nearby whom I found to be quite comforting as I wasn't entirely alone. In between my day and night jobs I had a few hours in which to walk about and take in the scene. I found an Irish pub and made friends with Jean the bartender. He was French Corsican but quite English in his mannerisms, he'd lived in England, Germany and France as well as Greece. He had a child and lived with the child's mother, but he was quite taken by me and told me that their relationship wasn't a committed one. Even so, we kept our attraction to each other quiet. He gave me free pints of Guinness at his pub. Over the weeks we formed a relationship, the attraction got the better of us. It was nothing serious, but it was undeniable. I washed my clothes at his house. He made me coffee with a splash of whiskey while I waited for the cycle to end, and we'd chat like old friends. Jean never judged me, he treated me with respect and saw me as a traveller experiencing life as opposed to a homeless person who'd lost their way. There was a mutual understanding between us. We both knew there was no future for us as a couple so enjoyed every moment as if it was the last. Our taste in music was uncannily similar and we bounced off each other's sense of humour. We danced alone where no one could see us and there were moments where we held each other like it was the last time ever.

He didn't like that I slept rough, but I didn't want to be beholden to anyone. He insisted I borrow his bicycle whilst I was going back and forth between jobs and the olive grove. It was a god send, it meant I had an hour longer to sleep. He looked after my guitar, I didn't have a lot of time to play it and had to focus mainly on work. It was tough but the only way forward.

Over the weeks I'd saved up enough money to get a coach from Athens back to the UK. Jean Paul was heading to France, so we decided to travel together and stop in France to see my dad for a couple of days. The journey was long, we passed through Italy, Austria and Belgium, we drank whisky for the whole of the trip. Had we stayed together I would have undoubtedly become an alcoholic. Our bond was special, it had the charm of a romantic story that only lasts a short time, or a love song, delicate and rare but cannot survive the world around it.

Dad and his girlfriend lived in a farmhouse on a large piece of land, with my 13-year old brother, Daniel. They had a pig, a sheep and 2 dogs. He wasn't in any position to help me out financially or put me up for long, but it was grounding and quite emotional to see them. The house was chaotic with the animals walking around freely indoors, like something out of a children's book. I kept my shoes on but would have been better off wearing wellies. It was in mid construction, but my thoughts were that it would never be finished. I bathed in a steel tin and the water was heated over the kitchen fire place.

Jean went with me to England by train to make sure I was back safe. It was a magical time. We didn't exchange contact details, I wanted a fresh start, Jean had his life and I had to sort out mine. We said our goodbyes at Paddington train station and that was the last time I ever saw him.

Chapter 5

There is so much reality in going home, facing truths, all the doubts and fears return, the memories and insecurities are still there and start to flow back into the forefront of your brain. Failures are magnified. Disappointment, expectations, guilt, shame, regret. A barrel of emotions all come flooding back and there you are in the middle of it all trying to start again. Nothing has changed, everything looks the same, the only difference is the experience you've faced during that time away. Nothing really to show for it, no qualifications or references, just stories and hopefully a bit more wisdom.

'Sparrow'

I sit and wonder in the light of day
Trees are still and the sky is grey
All the snow will soon be coming my way, and
I'll be lonely again
I wish that I had your wings to fly
I wish that I had your eyes

To see the world from the sky above.
I wish that I had your disguise.

Hey little sparrow in the tree
I know you are looking at me
Hey little sparrow, why do you stare?
When I've gone away will you still be there?

I walk and wander in the dark of night
Throw my worries to the wind
Like the ashes of an old friend
I say goodbye and walk away,
But they will always be a part of me,
Maybe sometimes on my mind.
I will live and I will learn from them
Memories never left behind

The Autumn breeze is now blowing all
The leaves like feathers in the air
I search the trees for you sparrow
But I can't see you anywhere
So, I turn and walk away again
Throw my worries to the wind
Like the ashes of an old friend
Maybe sometimes on my mind.

Coming back to my country was both comforting and daunting. It certainly highlighted the problems in my life. This was real. I had to face up to my failures and I had no idea where to start. Over time I had cut myself off emotionally from the people that cared about me. They had no idea how tough things had been for me. Had I tried to reach out for help at times and I'm sure had they known of the dangers I had faced they would have helped me out, but my shame had taken over. I blamed myself for my sorrows and the troubles I'd got myself into and had to try and correct things my way.

It was a frosty morning mid-November. I couldn't help but notice what a grey country England was in the winter. I stepped off the train in Henley with my guitar and rucksack, still wearing minimal light weight clothing and really feeling the cold. The sandals on my feet revealed my neglected toes which were weathered and hardened from walking barefoot for many months and a purple tinge was forming as the frost was biting into them. I couldn't remember the last time I bought a pair of socks, but this was the first thing on the list as soon as I got a job.

My brother, Patrick, lived in a 2 up 2 down semidetached house in Henley. He had inherited it from my English Grandmother who was still alive and still living on the land in Binfield heath where I grew up and where I had also lived for a while in the log cabin. Gran had owned the house in Henley which she rented to a single lady who had eventually died of old age and rather than rent it out again she gave it to my brother, Patrick, as he was now raising a family with his girlfriend Les. I got on well with Les, she was a lovely person that always saw the good in people. I felt sure that she would welcome me in when I turned up unannounced on their doorstep. I wasn't sure how Patrick would respond but I had nowhere else to go. Vicky would be the next choice but being a struggling single mum now I didn't want to burden her. I would see her the next day for sure and catch up on old times. Her little boy, Thomas, was my godson, and I couldn't wait to see how much he'd grown and give him a big hug. Patrick and Les's boy, Sam, was the same age, and they had another one on the way.

I stood at the door with a sense of unease, my father had probably warned them that I might turn up, but I wondered how they would feel about me being there, potentially relying on their hospitality for the unforeseeable future. Patrick and I had unresolved arguments and hostilities from poor miscommunication. Neither of us had coped well after the death of our mother and I didn't know if we were able to move past the fights and the cutting words that were thrown both ways. Whatever their first thoughts were when they invited me in, I think they were more concerned about the way I looked. I had barely seen myself. Survival had been my one and only priority and the fact that I'd made it back to my home town was nothing short of a miracle. If I hadn't visited the church and allowed myself to believe and have faith in something good out there, I would still be festering and wallowing in self-pity. Les made me a makeshift bed under the staircase and said I could stay until I got myself sorted. Patrick seemed alright about it too but was very busy working all the time on his business which was originally 'Watts Forestry'. He took the business over from Dad. He had big ideas and very innovatively grew the company into something much bigger. Patrick was an entrepreneur and within a short time he was on the threshold of owning a successful reputable plant hire company. He designed and built his own machines which he patterned and shipped all over the world.

In the evenings when Patrick had time we talked lots, bit by bit I gave him and Les small snippets of what had happened during my time away. There were things I was too ashamed about to share. I asked for my old job back at the Chef Peking and without any hesitation I got it. I cleaned myself up, stopped drinking and started a detox course. Within a few weeks I started to recognise the old me, the pre-destitute, healthy, level headed me. I'd combed the sun-bleached dreadlocks out of my hair, borrowed some makeup and smart clothes off Les to work in. I tried to be the perfect house guest, babysitting my nephew, helping with cooking and cleaning and trying not to be under their feet too much.

It was good to be home, Henley was home. People knew me. There was always someone there to help and listen and without the language barrier I felt I was no longer an outsider. I appreciated for the first time ever that sense of belonging, something I'd always taken for granted.

Life felt ok, looking after myself felt good but I needed to make plans. My job wasn't enough in the long term, and I couldn't stay at my brother's forever, so I had to come up with a plan.

I got in touch with Jane again. She was living in Sydney in a shared house and working in an office in the city. She was fairly settled but feeling restless and not particularly loving her job. She was missing the music and also missing me and desperate to get together to sing again. She had also contacted Simon from Greece, the one who I'd had a short romance with before he'd left to continue with his around the world travels. He was in India at the time, but his next stop was Thailand and then Australia. He was hoping to meet up with Jane as he would be flying into Sydney.

I'd thought about Simon quite a lot whilst in the depths of my despair wondering where he was in the world and if he'd met someone else or not. I wouldn't have been that bothered as I had never really imagined ever seeing him again but he'd asked Jane about me and had hoped I might come to Australia while he was there.

I wasn't sure how possible it would be. My job wasn't paying much, and I wasn't very good at saving. When I got the chance to mention it to Les she was full of encouragement. She got straight on the internet to find out the price of a return flight and said she would buy me the ticket and I could give her my wages at the end of each week until I'd paid her back. This was a great incentive, and I knew that it was the only way. I didn't have to pay any rent money and they provided me with a meal every day. It was definitely possible. All I needed next was a year's work permit. I was so excited, I got a train to London and queued up for hours until I was eventually seen and granted my visa.

It was early January, the weather was awful, and work was mundane, but I saved hard and got myself fit and healthy. I was running every day and trying to lose the debauched look from drinking far too much. I wouldn't have wanted Simon to see me the way I was when I'd returned from Greece, swollen faced, tired and dishevelled.

By the end of February, I was ready to go. I hadn't managed to save any more than £50 to take with me but the plan was to stay at Jane's for a while and look for a job. I wouldn't be in any worse position than where I was sleeping under the stairs at my brother's and washing up at the Chinese restaurant.

By the time I was ready to leave Simon had already got to Australia and phoned me up from Jane's house. It was the first time I'd heard his voice in about 6 months, and he told me over the phone that he never stopped thinking about me and couldn't wait to see me again.

Chapter 6

I boarded the plane, a shadow of the person I was a few months ago. My woes were far behind me, I had more confidence in myself and was looking good. This was going to be a new start. I put my rucksack and guitar in the overhead locker and settled into my seat, ready for the long journey to the other side of the world. For the first time in ages, I was feeling really positive.

The flight to Sydney was great, we stopped in Singapore and Abu Dhabi. I was intrigued by the time changes and whether the sun was coming up or going down. I must have been craving the feeling of the unknown, itchy feet maybe, but it felt great to be going away again away from the routine of the Chinese restaurant. I couldn't wait to see Jane and Simon. Before landing at Sydney airport, I tidied myself up a bit, applied some make up and brushed my hair.

Jane was waiting for me in arrivals. We threw our arms around each other, there's always that strange anticipation when seeing someone for the first time in ages but Jane and I just connected like no time at all had passed. Looking around me I was surprised how similar everything was to England, besides the heat and the sunshine. The city itself seemed familiar, similar shops and brands of products. People in suits rushing to work, coffee shops, restaurants, the same fashion, maybe a season behind or ahead, I couldn't quite work that out. Jane was living in the suburbs of Sydney, nice area, pretty houses all in the same style, spacious, open planned living space with large gardens at the back with decking.

I had no idea what to expect when I saw Simon. I didn't consider him to be my boyfriend, but I'd allowed myself to imagine we would run into each other's arms like in the films and be together again like we'd never parted. Time and events had numbed the earlier feelings I had towards him, but it was fun to dream. He was standing in the doorway when we pulled up in the drive. He was looking well-travelled, his freckles had joined up and he had a rosy glow about him. The big smile was still there, and his blue eyes stood out behind his sun-bleached straggly locks.

We hugged but it was like friends saying hi, a little awkward really. Maybe I had over thought things and was expecting to feel an immediate connection. Jane made tea and introduced me to her house mates. There was a sofa bed in the living room where Simon had been sleeping and I noticed there were no spare rooms so it was obviously assumed that I would either top and tail with Jane or share the sofa bed with Simon. I didn't worry too much about those details, but it did cross my mind briefly.

Jane was still working full time and although she had given in her notice so she could come travelling with me, she explained that she would have to work for another 2 months.

Writer's block is very real. I get frustrated and upset and wonder if my inspiration will ever return. As I wrote this song I realised myself that the muse is always there waiting for you to tune in but you have to have faith in it, in order to reconnect. 'The muse' is an entity in this song which helps me put a face to the inspirational force.

The Muse

Of all the hearts I would choose,
it would be a heart that's feeling torn and
bruised.
I'd leap over to October and lounge on a cloud
that's smoky grey.

You are the soul
I am the muse
we stumble and we're humble as a pair
I can not be seen,
you are not aware
that by your side is where I've always been.

I dawn from the dark of your broken heart,
like an animal that crawls out of a hole.
Is it right or is it wrong
that I celebrate my life in a song?

You are the soul,
I am the muse.
We stumble and we're humble as a pair.
I cannot be seen,
you are not aware
that by your side is where I've always been.

The dark nights have come
but summer hangs on,
like a leaf that holds tightly to a tree.
There is something in the air,
a certain kind of melancholy.

I don't mourn or cry
I fly above the roof top late at night.
I'll be there in your mind,
when you wake up, I will be there by your side.

Simon was working in a cafe and doing long daytime shifts, so I found myself alone a lot during the day. I searched for jobs in the city and the suburbs but didn't even get an interview. I was down to my last few pennies.

I knew that once Jane had done her notice, we could go busking but until then I was a little lost. I had to be patient, everything was new, and it felt a little daunting. People were busy with their lives, and I didn't know how to start mine on the other side of the world.

As a song writer boredom has very rarely been a thing for me. I've always been comfortable in my own company, as long as I have a guitar and a pen. If I had nothing to write, I would draw. Now I found myself sitting in the perfect house on a perfect street, food in the fridge and beautiful weather and I was bored. I couldn't find words in my head or tunes or pictures. I went for walks, ate mangos and bathed in the sun. One morning when everyone had gone to work, I lay on the sofa bed contemplating what to do with my day. The prospect of more job hunting was killing me. I was broke and couldn't afford to go into the city and there was nothing anywhere local, I'd searched far and wide.

I got up and went to have a shower but stopped in my tracks as I noticed there was a pair of scissors in the bathroom, so I decided to trim my fringe and put some layers in my hair. I hadn't cut it for a long time, and it was still bleached from living in Greece and hanging well below my shoulders. It was a part of myself that I liked. As I was cutting through, I felt a mixture of excitement and fear, my heart was racing and the scissors started to snip in time with the beat, snip, snip, snip. I kept cutting and laughed to myself. By the end there was nothing but blond tufts. I grabbed some hair gel and ran it through, pulling it into short spikes. Standing back from the mirror I realised I looked like a boy.

Jane was aghast when she came home that evening, but Simon loved the new look. I was still excited, I felt like a new person. We opened a bottle of vodka and decided to party that night. It was the end of the week, and I was pleased to finally have some company. Simon and I hadn't discussed our relationship or the prospect of it happening again, and I realised that it was probably just being in Greece, partying every night and just being swept along with the whole holiday romance thing. I didn't try to start anything and neither did he. I shared Jane's room until Simon went to work in the mornings and then I would lie in the warm space where he slept on the sofa bed before deciding what to do with my day. I must have been attracted to him still but didn't know how to reignite the flame. Jane introduced me to the music of Australian rock band Cold Chisel. We downed neat vodka shots and danced around the room.

Later that night Jane went off to bed and left Simon and me to chat. We talked about Greece, and he told me that he hadn't stopped thinking about me. One thing led to another and by the morning we were kind of together again. He decided to leave his job in the cafe and the two of us would go on a short travelling adventure together while Jane finished her notice at work. About 250 km west of Sydney was a place we'd heard of where people went to pick fruit. Anyone could go there and get work. It was a farming community that grew produce for the whole of Australia.

I still had a week with nothing to do but walk and eat mangos in between sunbathing and making cups of tea. Sounds like bliss but I needed something constructive or creative to do. My guitar sat alone, sad and neglected, I didn't feel inspired to play and I needed new strings which I couldn't afford. I felt a bit out of sorts, no direction and a little weary. Looking in the mirror at my new pixie hair cut depressed me a bit, the novelty had worn off, I didn't feel like me anymore. I had the type of hair that would naturally curl so when it was short it just bent and kinked in all directions and had a habit of looking frizzy sometimes. I decided I needed a hat. I knew exactly the type I wanted but I wouldn't find one in the suburbs of Sydney, and I had barely a penny to my name. I came up with an idea. When Jane and the others got home from work that day, I asked them if they had any spare clothes that they wanted to get rid of. Without any questions they disappeared into their rooms, and each came out with an armful of things. From denim jeans, flowery cotton shirts to fluorescent pink and green polyester shorts and paisley satin blouses. The perfect multi-coloured feast of potential hats. I chopped off all the bits I didn't want and laid out large squares which I then halved, then quartered and finally sewed them all together to make one large sheet of patchwork. The following day I bought some cheap elastic, cut the fabric into circles, lined them with plain fabric and seamed all around the edge so I could feed the elastic through. I made the peaks out of ice-cream lids which I covered with denim and joined them to the berets. I ended up with bright multicoloured floppy hats. Perfect for hiding my short, unkempt hair and achieving a more bohemian look. The compliments never stopped, and I was soon asked to make them for other people. The week flew by and I was satisfied with my achievements. I had invented a new me, keeping the old bits that I liked, and I was ready to hit the road.

Man, and a van. (Not yet recorded)

The clapped-out van has broken down
The heaven's opened wide
Inches from the ditch
I fear we're going to fall inside
Don't know where we are
Or what we're going to do
But I know I'm stuck here next to you.

Who said love was supposed to be
A picnic in the sun
Blanket by the riverside
Having lots of fun
Ice-cream cones and
Champagne just for two
That's not how it's meant to be with you.

Paper coffee cups will do
And ready salted crisps.
Life is good, we have a roof
Even though it drips
If I could I'd do it all again
There's nothing I would ever want to change.

Who said love was meant to be
A picnic in the park
Diamond rings and violins
Candles in the dark
Ice-cream cones
Champagne just for two
That's not how it's meant to be with you.

Ok before you start imagining that we drove to Griffith in a van, I'll stop you there. Writing an autobiography for me is digging up everything that I can remember, filtering out some unimportant stuff, leaving out certain amounts of detail but giving the reader a true unexaggerated version of events.

The beauty of being a song writer, however, is doing the opposite, including the fantasy, writing the parts that the imagination conjures up and allowing the listener to step inside that fictional story, to let them relate to it in some way. Like painting a picture and the observer seeing what they want to see and feeling what they want to feel. A song can take you to a place where it can open the creative mind. I try to keep things impersonal but most of my songs do indeed stem from my own experiences. Simon and I first met whilst slumming it in a Greek hovel of a hostel and that pattern was to continue. The 'van' like a hypothetical bubble was our safe place, it wasn't perfect or romantic in the conventional sense; it was fragile, there were cracks, holes and blemishes but it withheld a great partnership for that short time and made a sweet memory.

Whilst we were staying in the clean, safe, functional house which was Jane's in Sydney, we felt disconnected and confused as to what exactly our relationship was but when we left together on our adventure, we found that connection again. Our relationship was never going to survive conformity 'Man and a van' is about a relationship that thrives on dysfunctional bliss. Unfortunately, we didn't have a van in the literal sense, but the lyrics tell a semi fictional tale and describe a feeling from a memorable time in my life.

Simon lent me some money to get a Greyhound ticket which I would pay him back for once we started earning. We travelled through the night, inland from Sydney and arrived in a town called Griffith at about 4 am. It was still dark and freezing cold, it felt like an English winter which we weren't prepared for, and the place looked deserted.

I was desperate for a cup of coffee. I don't think I got any sleep on the bus and my tiredness only made the cold I felt more intense. We walked to keep warm and waited for the sun to rise and at least one shop or cafe to open. The high street was dead and there were no signs of anything opening soon.

I had heard so many great things about Australia but I'd yet to find them. My vision was Crocodile Dundee/Mad Max hats with corks and Castle Maine 4X. This definitely wasn't either of those things but here I was, and I was going to make the most of it.

The sun rose bright in the cloudless sky like a giant radiator warming up the crumbly red earth beneath my feet. Droplets of morning dew evaporated into a hazy mist and there were the morning sounds of bird song along with busying shop owners opening their doors. Still the roads were quiet and there was just Simon and me filled with relief to be welcomed inside the only supermarket on the high street. We each bought a pint of milk to keep us going and set off to explore, find work and a campsite. We picked up a two-man tent for 19 dollars. It was basic, but I still had no money and Simon was on a tight budget, but we figured it would do us. By about 9 am the town started to get busier, and we spotted a couple of travellers. They had that bohemian look about them, scruffy, hippy style clothing and dreadlocks. Looked like they'd been on the road for some time in a rundown old VW. Within 5 minutes of talking to them we got all the information we needed. By the end of the day, we had somewhere to pitch our tent and a job starting the next day. It wasn't quite how we imagined as we thought we'd be staying on a campsite but instead we pitched our tent in a barn on a farm. The barn was empty but had been used for livestock, it had an old trough in there with a shower attached which only had cold running water, but it was better than nothing. We were grateful for having a roof over our heads, even if you could see the sunlight shining through it. Our tent was very flimsy and might not have stood the cold, frosty nights and biting wind. The farmer gave us extra blankets and a thin mattress, and we made the tent into a cosy bedroom within the barn. We managed to also borrow a gas stove, so we were well sorted.

Work started at 8 am and we were shown around an orange grove. Strapping the pouches around us we began to pick the fruit, placing them in the pouch until it was full then we would empty it into the trailer and repeat all day until 6 pm. The mid-day sun had us sweating profusely and our thirst was unquenchable. We worked really hard and were totally exhausted by the end of the day. The farmer worked out how much we had earned by how much fruit was collected and it was a ridiculously small amount of money. He explained that to earn more we needed to work much faster. The next day we were hurting all over but continued picking, frantically. We watched a couple of Japanese lads that had mastered the job so artfully, climbing and swinging through the trees with the heavy sacks. They made it look so easy with their long lean arms and nimble athletic torsos. They were on triple the money we were making. We persevered and got better as the week went on. Very soon we got into the way of farm living. We visited the campsite nearby which was full of pickers and did swaps for different fruits and vegetables. Every evening after a cold shower we made vegetable stew from the produce we'd collected. Each week we moved to different fields. We soon learned the art of picking grapes, pumpkins and water melons. We became strong, tanned and very lean but it was tough and unsustainable. My hands bled every day and I regularly suffered from heat exhaustion from working in extreme temperatures. At night, although it was close to freezing, by mid-day it would sometimes reach 42°. We never really consumed enough water but would get juice from the melons. There wasn't much to do in the evenings, and we were too tired to do anything other than eat and sleep, so we saved a bit of money and killed a bit of time before returning back to Sydney. Jane was soon to complete her notice and would be ready to begin her travels.

The experience was good. We were thankful to the farmer for giving us work and a place to stay for free, but it was time to leave and start a new adventure. It had been good spending time with Simon, but I wasn't sure that there could be a future for us. We got on great, but it wasn't enough, I needed to find myself and explore Australia without the complications of a serious relationship.

Autumn in Sydney was very different from England, the beach was still littered with bodies. People were in shorts and t-shirts and the outside bars were bustling with young folk and live bands, there were no signs yet of hatching down for the winter months. I did feel a sense of end of holiday though as schools and colleges were back, and very soon there would be a change in the season and the weather would start to get cold.

Jane was excited to see me. She had stopped work and we all began to party again like old times at Pythagoras in the old town of Rhodes. Out came the vodka shots and on came the music. After a few drinks I stuck on a floppy hat and Jane and I went out for a pizza to discuss travel plans. Simon's plan was to head up to Byron Bay and meet up with friends. We agreed to part company for a while so Jane and I could catch up properly and work on our music, busking and searching for gigs. Simon and I didn't officially break up, so we kept the choice of the unknown open. There was plenty of opportunity to reunite sometime down the track.

I still had a nagging urge to see if Crocodile Dundee land and the Mad Max underground world actually existed. Jane wanted to introduce me to her friends and family in Canberra, so we included that into the plan and bought 2 Greyhound tickets to travel where ever we wanted on the east side of Australia and up the centre.

Canberra, the Australian capital territory was pretty much as I imagined - clean, modern, not a lot of character but very functional and idyllic, some very pretty parts with a river and woodland and places to go wild swimming with picnic and barbecue spots but the city itself was drenched with newness and capitalism. It was a pleasure to meet Jane's family as I'd heard so much about them. We spent 2 days exploring the best parts of Canberra and the final day we went to a festival of live bands, that was the highlight for me. The next day we were off on our long-awaited adventure of a life time.

I'd never been a big fan of coaches, but the Greyhound was fairly spacious. It had a big bull bar on the front for obvious reasons, driving through the outback where wild animals are abundant and traffic very light. They tend to wander around freely. I spotted a few dead kangaroos on the side of the road. I felt sad to see those large beautiful marsupials lying there alone rotting in the intense heat of the Australian outback, I could almost imagine the smell. I wondered how long they would be there in one piece before being swooped upon by Wedge tailed eagles or such birds.

The road was long, wide and dusty, there was nothing to see but miles and miles of red earth and scrubland. The odd little cluster of scantily built residencies barely habitable in the extreme dry heat except for maybe a creek which would hopefully supply fresh water.

It was a long 7-hour journey and I made myself sleep to pass the time. Drifting in and out of dreams with the warmth of the sun on the window, I found myself quite enjoying the relaxing experience. I was excited when I saw the first signpost for Melbourne and the closer we got, the more civilisation we started to see, a petrol station, a truck stop, bill boards. I had wondered what would have happened had we broken down, but I tried not to dwell on that too much, just glad to be close to safe surroundings again.

Melbourne in my imagination was like Neighbours, Ramsey Street, perfect little housing estates with balconies and outdoor pools, beautiful tanned people and plenty of sunshine. In reality it was like England without the quirkiness, a tram running through the city instead of black taxis and red buses. It rained solidly for 3 days, and it was cold and grey. The hostel was basic, and we were hugely outnumbered by wealthy Chinese students with their expensive cameras. The methodical way they prepared and cooked food put us to shame. Jane and I perfected the art of cooking 2-minute noodles and clearing up within 3 minutes, managing not to get in anyone's way. We made friends with a girl who was travelling alone or rather she found us and stuck to us like a limpet. When we went busking, she came with us, talked endlessly, moaned continuously about the cold and was constantly hungry. Her idea to become travelling companions was never going to happen, her naivety and unworldliness would have weighed us down. We were hardened adventurers open to all eventualities and expectant of potential disasters. Busking to us was work, up at sunrise, mug of strong coffee and out the door grabbing a bread roll and a banana on the way before finding the perfect spot in the busiest part of the city. Jane and I got our voices working so well together, our phrasing was perfect and our harmonies came naturally where sometimes we would automatically switch without knowing it; it was like we could read each other, the girl in the hostel wanted to be a part of it but it was too precious to us and so was our friendship. Sometimes in life you make selfish decisions. We couldn't really accommodate the girl into our lives as she wanted, so instead, we moved on. We had a few good days and nights out in Melbourne before jumping back on the Greyhound to Adelaide.

It never ceased to astonish me how big and vast Australia was. We travelled mostly by night so slept a lot, but the journey was approximately 12 hours. There wasn't a lot of difference between the cities, not from a busker's point of view. I'm sure for a tourist that was sightseeing they would find that Adelaide had more culture about it. The buildings looked interesting. We only stayed a couple of nights, the mall was similar, there were some trendy shops and bars etc. but we barely explored. City life was difficult, it was hard to know where to go and play, there is a certain etiquette with street musicians, it's not really cool to step on someone else's turf.

The weather was on the turn, and we were spending more money than we were making so the decision to make our next big move was the right one.

Looking at the map of Australia in the bus station scared me and excited me at the same time. We had come about as far as we could along the south coast before reaching the boundary over to the west side of the country where our bus tickets would not be valid so rather than go back on ourselves there only one other way to go. Up through the red centre towards Darwin. Feeling a shiver from the cool southern autumn air and contemplating paying for another night in a hostel, it seemed like a no brainer to jump on a bus and sleep through the 9-hour night journey to Coober Pedy....Mad Max territory!

Had I not been shockingly awoken by the thud of a wild suicidal scrub bull I might have slept through the whole journey. For a moment during my disorientation, I thought we'd crashed and fallen into a ditch but then I realised we were travelling along a straight road in the Australian desert, we would be lucky to even see a creek. I managed to doze for a bit until the sun, like a big red apple started to appear on the horizon; it was the only focal point within a huge expanse of nothingness.

Within minutes I felt like I was in a painting. The sky was on fire, streaks of orange and red crudely brushed across a canvas. It was like the artist had run out of other colours. Not a tree in sight; we had been travelling for hours in the dark, I hadn't seen a single other vehicle. Why had that bull chosen that moment earlier to cross the road? I wondered.

Me, on my bunk, in the underground hostel in Coober Pedy

Coober Pedy, opal capital of the world. The sign stood out, glowing in the middle of the red desert but it was about all that stood out except for lots of poles with signs dotted about and a few roofs jutting out of the ground. Initially I was disappointed, what was this place that we were disembarking the bus for? It was a long way to the next stop, and I needed to stretch my legs and eat so we decided to stay a night or two. I wondered what the attraction was. From what I could see this could be the most uninteresting place I'd ever been and what if we got stranded? A Greyhound strike maybe or a cyclone warning?

First impressions can be deceiving. We found a hostel, it was basically a cave; it was fully equipped but it was literally underground. This wasn't just a hostel, it was more like a museum! The sense of relief I felt as I lay on my bunk was a memory I will never forget. The walls around me were stone and I could feel the coolness in the unconditioned air as opposed to the intense heat outside. There was just about enough room on the top bunk of my bed to sit cross legged without banging my head on the uneven curvature of stone above me, so I grabbed my guitar, smiled to myself and played.

The next morning, we woke up and decided to venture out, we were too exhausted to check out the night life the previous evening and didn't want to spoil the inspiring moment of cave life which we had not expected the evening before. Stepping out, squinting into the morning sun reminded us that sunglasses were a must. It was the desert but this was a city and all those bill boards and signs on poles led to underground shops, bars, cafés and restaurants. This was possibly the most fascinating place I'd ever been. Not particularly nice or even enjoyable but like nowhere else I'd ever been. We found a supermarket, Woolworths of course. Everything was stacked in the same format as every other Woolworths even though we felt like we were on another planet. I couldn't decide whether the normality and familiarity of that was a comfort or a disappointment but nevertheless we managed to easily find our usual bread rolls and bananas. Grabbing a few other things we decided to cook a healthy meal in the hostel kitchen that evening.

Jane and I, throughout all our travelling adventures and experiences, had become quite spiritual, not in the biblical sense but having done a séance in Greece we strongly believed that there was more out there than we are supposed to be aware of. When you can't make sense of something because it's unclear and unproven the only thing to do is to believe in the thing that comforts you and makes you feel safe. We were both lost souls I suppose, young, unworldly and finding our way, exploring our thoughts and beliefs. Our only real focus at the time was our music, neither of us had particular goals or ambitions that didn't involve music in some way. We were creative free-spirited day dreamers, and it made sense to us to have spirit guides. My guide was my deceased Mother. We believed in signs and were very intuitive. Everything we did and most decisions we made were having followed a sign. We followed our every instinct and allowed ourselves to trust in them. It was a wonderful way to live as we feared very little.

There was a reason for everything that happened and between our guides and the universe each day was mapped out for us; one event led to another.

Walking back from the supermarket that day we noticed in the distance a cross on top of what seemed to be a big rock, probably once an opal mine. We wandered up to it and discovered it was an underground church. There was a sign on the door with opening times and services. Making a mental note we agreed to attend the Sunday morning service the next day before heading off further north.

After dinner and a couple of beers in the hostel Jane and I sat on our bunk and played a few songs before falling asleep. It was easy to sleep in the cool, dark cave of the dormitory. There weren't any of the usual noisy party types and nobody objected to us doing a bit of music.

Sunday morning after breakfast we slung on a pair of shorts, vest and sandals, slapped on a hat and headed off to church. I had my guitar on my back as I would never leave it. It wasn't really of much monetary value, but it was how we made our living, and we couldn't afford to lose it.

It appeared to be very quiet when we arrived at the church, but the door was open, so we wandered in. It had that usual smell of frankincense mixed with an earthy scent. There were candles lit which glowed against the rust coloured rock. On wooden benches sat casually dressed people of all ages.

The lady Reverend held out her arms towards us as we stood at the entrance looking and feeling a little awkward. Her face lit up as she spotted my guitar and after a few minutes of introductions she asked us if we would kindly play something at the end of her sermon.

The service was lovely, softly spoken like an angel. The Reverend told some beautiful stories. I enjoy listening to the words from the bible, knowing that they are such ancient words, having been told and read through so many generations by so many people. The purity and goodness in that cave like church was calming and warm. I was a little nervous at the prospect of singing to the congregation, but it was one of those callings that we felt honoured to do and another crazy, wonderful story to tell others and to remember forever. The faces in front of us were warm and welcoming, accepting of the very unexpected duo that had randomly appeared from nowhere. It was without question which song we would perform, our most polished, entirely appropriate internationally known song by Simon and Garfunkel. As I lightly picked the intro on my guitar, smiles of recognition appeared on friendly faces, the acoustics in the room could echo the sound of a pin dropping. I was thankful to myself for having recently changed my strings and to my unusually steady hand in such nerve-wracking situations. Apart from the sound of my guitar, the room was silent within the glow of candle light and finally, with such perfected harmonies we sang the words, 'Hello darkness my old friend'.

Most people stop at Coober Pedy to buy opals or see the mines, possibly intrigued by the underground living, others stop for a break on their way to Ayres rock or up to the Northern territory. We went to church!

The thing about being off the beaten track, not following what the tourists do or what the guide book suggests is seeing a real part of the community and taking something special from it, a memory that is unique, and what better way than being in the very heart of that community. That day we also left a small part of ourselves, we made people smile with our presence and we left an echo of a song resonating within the cool walls of that cave 'The sound of silence'.

Our next stop, off the Greyhound up through the red centre was Uluru national park. 7 hours of desert to get there but I would sleep it. We were getting used to long journeys, I would roll a hoody into an oblong pillow shape and wrap it around my neck to support my head and doze off. It was quite pleasant stepping up onto the air-conditioned bus and having nothing to do but relax with the sun's warm rays on my face against the window. There were occasional fuel stops where we'd freshen up for 10 minutes before heading back to the bus and resuming our previous positions.

We were now very much in the thick of the Great Victoria desert. I no longer worried about breaking down, I'd put my concerns to bed. It's like when you board a plane for the first time in ages you think of the worst possible scenarios. This was getting easy, sleep, wake, toilet break, repeat. Along the way we spotted some very remote aboriginal villages. I was quite shocked to see the poverty as we passed through such areas. Half-clad children walking about unattended waving at us through the bus window but what really got to me was how many flies congregated around their little faces, sapping at the moisture from their mouths, nose and eyes. They didn't seem to be in the least bit bothered though. I was thankful to be on the bus travelling well away from it all.

I slept for the final leg of the journey and woke up as the Greyhound came to a halt in Uluru. I stretched and yawned, gathered my bits together and made my way to the exit, looking forward to some civilization. I didn't know much about the place only that it was home to Ayres Rock which we were planning to climb. What I hadn't anticipated were the flies. I witnessed it way back on the journey through the window but wasn't expecting to arrive into a swarm of them. It was worse than I possibly could have imagined. Of course, we were completely unprepared. Everyone we saw wore nets which covered their whole heads. We had to get from the bus to a shop that supplied these special hats and in the mean time we were being eaten, not by one but about 30 blue and black buzzing little creatures. We could keep our mouths closed but our eyes were almost blinded by the hideous things. Apart from Desert all that was there were a few shops, a hotel and a hostel. I was a little daunted at first, but we got the nets, checked into the hostel and searched the shops for some food. A tin of tuna and some bread rolls was what we decided on but when we sat at a picnic bench to prepare our lunch, we realised how stupid we were. We had invited the whole community of Uluru's flies to join us. It was impossible to eat, and we were starving. A lesson learned, we stayed inside the hostel until the next day when we bit the bullet, put on our bee keeper type hats and went on our exploration of Ayres rock, our first real touristic experience.

From a distance it didn't look that big but as we got to the base, I almost started having regrets, the temperature was up in the 40's. I love climbing and walking but in reality, what was there to actually see once at the top but miles and miles of nothing, but miles and miles.

My only incentive was, having talked to some lads that had just come back down, that there were no flies up the top. That was enough to make me want to run up there. Unfortunately, it wasn't as simple as that. It was a long way up, we couldn't see the top. Every time we saw a ledge and thought we were getting close there would be another steep bit beyond. We had just about enough water with us, but I'd never felt so hot and exhausted, it was almost soul destroying, but Jane urged me to keep going and we did. We made it to the top and stripped off our vests and jumped around with joy. Those lads were right, there were no flies!

Coming back down was easy and fun. We needed to be at the base before sunset as that was when the rock was at its reddest. The sun sets at 6 or 7pm in Australia depending on where you are and within minutes the day turns to night.

We stood from a far enough distance away to appreciate the full width of the rock and as we waited for the sun to set, we watched it turn from a rusty orange to the brightest, richest red imaginable, it was quite surreal and a totally magical experience.

So, I climbed Ayres rock and have the photo to prove it, semi naked from the top, dancing around in the midday sun 360° view of nothing but space. How can such an expanse of nothingness look so beautiful? I wanted to fly like a bird of prey into the streak less cloud free sky.

Back at the hostel that night we tucked into some cheesy nachos and a box of Riesling, we'd earned it. There was music going on in the court yard, chaps with a guitar and a didgeridoo, I grabbed mine and we joined them. One thing I noticed about the sun going down is that the flies go to bed. We were in Uluru, Australia's red centre, singing traditional Aussi folk songs with a couple of Mick Dundee lookalikes. I had finally arrived!

We were planning to move on the next day but got talked into seeing the Olga's, a rock formation, sacred to the aborigines. Again lots of walking but whilst there we got to experience some mind-blowing rock art and dream time stories. I felt like a tourist, but it felt good, I needed to learn something about the country I had landed on, other than the fictional shows I'd watched on TV.

Another day, another adventure.

Having secured in my mind the fact that we were indeed heading in the right direction, far away from the southern Australian winter, I settled back into my seat on the Greyhound mentally preparing myself for a long 20-hour journey up to Darwin. There were a couple of cities along the way, one being Alice Springs where we spent a night. The spring was dry, there had been a drought, but we found a bar where there was a band playing. It was a pleasant stop over but not ideal for busking. I was eager to get to Darwin. I still hadn't seen any hats with corks, although I think they'd been replaced with nets. Crocodiles and snakes were also on the agenda; until I'd seen them in in their natural habitat I hadn't quite arrived.

Again, I was relieved to be back in the air-conditioned bus and drifted into sleep mode. The journey seemed endless as I dozed in and out of strange dreams, occasionally looking out of the window at nothing, finding my time bearings by the position of the sun. Day turned to night and there was nothing but the moon and the stars to look at. I unravelled my hoodie from behind my neck as the air-conditioning started to bother me. All I had on were shorts and a vest, so I snuggled up inside the fleecy lining and allowed my head to rest against the window. A few hours later I awoke to Jane shivering beside me. She too was underdressed and considered asking the driver if there were any blankets. She was freezing, I felt it too and pulled my hoodie over my goose pimpled legs. Looking around I noticed people pulling out items of clothing from their travel bags. We were travelling through a state of Australia where it rarely drops below 20° even at night. As Jane and I huddled up to keep warm the driver spoke through the microphone explaining that the air-conditioning had mal functioned, and we would stop at the next city so we could get warm items out of the storage hold. I'm sure there was ice on the insides of the windows by the time we arrived in Katherine. As we shivered our way off the bus the warm night air hit us. I wanted to curl up on the pavement and go to sleep, anything but get back on that bus, it was literally an ice box. I travelled extremely lightly but managed to find a pair of jeans and layered my top half up with every t-shirt I had. Jane did the same. The more sensible travellers had sleeping bags, pyjamas, tracksuits, every survival item for every adverse situation imaginable. The final few hours of the journey went slowly. It was impossible to sleep as we froze through the rest of the journey.

Arriving in Darwin at 6 am was more than a huge relief. We were cold to the bone, hungry and tired. I needed coffee. The bus pulled into the station, the doors opened, and the warm morning air was bliss. Of all the scenarios I'd imagined it was never the possibility of freezing to death in the Australian outback.

Darwin had the usual civilisation of any other small Australian city, a little run down in places. Houses were built on stilts in 1974 after cyclone Tracy hit and wiped out 80% of the city.

The street was quiet, nothing was open yet as we followed directions to the nearest hostel. Luckily someone was there manning the reception, we checked in and lay down on our simple, plain, white sheeted beds for a while. I noticed there was no air-conditioning which for once I was quite thankful for but as the sun rose, it started to feel sticky in our small very basic dorm. The ceiling fan didn't bring much relief either and I hoped that it wouldn't take too long for us to acclimatise to these conditions. It was from one extreme to another. We planned to stay in Darwin for at least a few weeks as we needed to settle down and start earning some money.

Life in Darwin wasn't without stress. There was a mentality there that made us feel like we'd stepped back into the 1970's, the tropical heat must have slowed everyone down. The smell of marijuana was prevalent just walking down the road or sitting on a bench in the park. There were large groups of aboriginal people congregating under trees with beer or cider. Even business people ambled along in their shorts and shirts in a relaxed, sedate manner on their way to the office.

The mall was pretty with well-kept flower beds. The daily hour of rain in the wet season kept them watered. Many people sat under the shade of the parasol like trees leisurely enjoying their lunch outside. We found our spot by a circle of benches and set up each day to entertain the lunchers and the passersby; it was perfect. Darwin accepted us and we soon became a small part of the community.

We moved into an apartment for a while which over looked the square where there were regular performers playing on small stage. We secured ourselves a gig with full PA and put posters and leaflets around the town. Before too long we started making friends with the locals as well as other travellers.

Hamish was an Irish juggler that busked in town. He had his own spot where he would stand, surrounded usually by a bunch of kids, fascinated by the way he spun his batons through the air. We passed him every day on our way to our patch. He admired my hat and put an order in for something similar but bigger, floppier and more colourful. It took me a week to make it. Finding the brightest, boldest pieces of fabric I stitched it all together, lining it with buttercup yellow satin. The finished product was every colour of the rainbow. I felt so proud handing it to him and seeing his face light up but a little sad to part with it. It was my best one yet.

Throughout our stay in Darwin, I got myself into some silly situations. Taking a long walk one day I found a path that led down to the sea, a quiet little cove where I thought I could go for a quick dip to cool off. I didn't see the crocodile sign and waded into the water. Taking long strokes I swam out enjoying the tranquillity of being by myself. As I floated on my back looking up at the cloudless sky, a voice in the distance startled me - a man shouting and running fully clothed into the sea with waving arms. He was bounding towards me, splashing awkwardly in a panic like state through the shallow water. I thought about ignoring him, but his tone was becoming angry, and I realised it must be a private beach or something. "Crocodiles," he shouted. As I started swimming back to shore, he repeatedly shouted obscenities at me as it finally hit me what he was trying to warn me about. I was swimming in crocodile infested waters! I had an incredibly lucky escape and my first lesson about living in a country where humans are potentially on the menu. Yes, I wanted to see crocodiles but not be eaten by one.

Another thing I learnt about Darwin was the number of alcoholics and drug addicts around. There were many young runaways that hid out there, sleeping rough and getting dragged into the dangerous underworld of heroin addiction.

I met a man called Richard who was quite attractive, well dressed and seemingly intelligent. We spent a night together drinking wine and talking for hours until the sun came up. Very soon we became quite close spending every bit of time we could together. I was intrigued by his slightly mysterious ways. I could see myself falling for him but at the same time trying to stay focused on the relationship I had with Simon and the fact that we were planning on meeting up again sometime down the track so with Richard I decided to try and stay within the friend zone. One day though he and I got into one of those arguments where you have no idea how it happened but certain that you hadn't started it. I submitted, apologising for my part in it, desperate to avoid confrontation but he turned on me in the most verbally aggressive way. Not making any sense at all. Spitting incoherent words at me. I felt scared and unsafe, I'd been here before with Evan. Recognising the signs of an unstable person with obvious mental health problems, I started to walk away, trying to stay calm but he followed me, speeding up his pace and shouting the most abusive, threatening words at me. I started to run, looking for help, searching everywhere for Jane. I made it back home, but Jane wasn't there. I locked the door behind me as he thundered up the stairs towards my apartment. For hours he kicked and kicked the door, shouting, banging, threatening until eventually the noise finally stopped and everything went quiet. Shaking with fear I cautiously unlocked and opened the door, stepping over him, lying dishevelled and unconscious on the floor. Later I discovered he was a heroin addict. Never would I have guessed. He hid his addiction behind his smartly dressed and eloquently spoken mannerisms. I managed to avoid him for the rest of the week. He must have taken off somewhere or hid himself away. I felt sad as I was becoming quite fond of that person, but I didn't feel safe anymore. I have no idea what it is about me that attracts people like that. Richard knew where I was living and Darwin wasn't a big enough place to not be found so after a bit of thought and contemplation, we decided it was time to move on.

Before we planned our next stop, we decided to take the opportunity whilst up in the Northern territory to visit Kakadu national park. Some friends were driving there so we hitched a ride with them and camped in the bush. There were tours and boat trips. It was where most of Crocodile Dundee was filmed. It was good to have that break. I was a little shaken up after what had happened in Darwin and I needed to clear my head before getting back on track, ready to continue the busking on new turf.

Same tune

I love your smile when you're smiling at me, I love your laugh when you're laughing with me and when I sigh, you're sighing with me and when I cry, you're crying with me.

You catch me falling when I fall too deep, you hear me calling when I call in my sleep and when I'm losing, losing my mind I know you're bruising and you're hurting inside.

I know your feet and how we step in time, I know your arms, how they swing like mine, I know your hips, how they move with the groove, I know your lips, how they sing the same tune.

It's strange but it's real what I feel when I'm with you, it's surreal but I feel like we're singing the same tune.

Travelling had become me. When things go wrong, move on. I was no longer running away; I was running to something, another story, another song. New places, different faces. Our next home was to be Cairns and our office, the shopping mall. Jane and I had become so in tune with each other, we were almost like a married couple, not just in the way that we protected each other, we started to think the same, walk, talk and sing almost in unison. We argued too but not for long. When one of us was feeling low, the other was too. We carried each other through our ups and downs as we stumbled along aimlessly.

Having experienced our longest Greyhound journey yet, approximately 28 hours, we were glad and relieved to arrive in Cairns, north Queensland, Australia's gateway to the Great Barrier Reef. Having had time to reflect, I realised that I missed Simon. We kept in contact through PO box, which was a little difficult, but I was aware through his last letter that he was currently visiting the Great Barrier Reef and staying at a hostel in Cairns. I was really looking forward to seeing a familiar, friendly face. We never talked about our relationship being exclusive neither did we plan to meet other partners. Travelling to us both was about being open to all opportunities. However, after the previous encounter in Darwin which could have been something but fortunately wasn't really, I felt a new excitement about reuniting with my old flame.

We checked into the hostel on the Esplanade where Simon was staying and waited around on sunbeds in the courtyard. He could have been anywhere, maybe even moved on but luckily, we caught him that afternoon returning from a boat trip. His blond hair even longer and scruffier, he started to look like an Australian surfer. He beamed as he spotted us, and we fell into a group hug. It was so good to see him. The three of us went for coffee and Simon showed us around the small but vibrant coastal town.

It was tourist heaven, clubs, bars, boats and back packers taking a gap year with lots of money. Maybe if we had money, we could be like the rest of them and explore all the fun things to do but we needed to work. I couldn't even afford the hostel that night. So before putting food in our mouths we had to go and start earning. Jane afforded us both the coffee which was like a meal in our empty stomachs and the three of us chatted, exchanging stories and adventures. Tired from our journey we freshened up back at the hostel before heading out to earn our keep.

Busking can be tough at times, singing the same set over and over for hours on end, being stared at, humiliated, told to move, even pitied. One lady in Cairns put a measly dollar in my guitar case with a sorrowful look on her face saying, "You're some mother's daughters." We actually managed to laugh about that. Never did we see ourselves as beggars. We were street musicians, and we were supplying a service to the public. Thankfully we were mostly appreciated but comments like that can be cutting and confidence destroying.

Our first day at the mall went well, we paid for our accommodation and had some more money left for food and beer. The next day would be better as we'd start in the morning and work all day.

By the end of our first week in Cairns we had made enough money to have some time off and relax for a few days. We had made friends with some Christian lads that had a juice bar in the mall. It was a converted van which they served freshly squeezed orange juice from. These men were young with long hair and beards. They wore white robes, looking like they'd stepped out of a picture bible. They were extremely friendly and enjoyed our music. When they invited us to stay at their abode in the mountains we jumped at the offer as it would give us a break from paying the hostel as well as food, as they offered to provide us with that too.

Simon, Jane and I stepped aboard their van on the Friday evening after work and we set off to their beautiful woodland place about an hour's drive away near Gillies range. They had a very modest, simply equipped but spacious house, surrounded by trees and a couple of static caravans in the woods for guests to stay in, one for men, the other for women. These chaps had a worldliness about them, like they had seen and experienced a lot, but they also seemed troubled and damaged in some way. Inside the house were pictures of Jesus on the walls. There were lots of books and bibles, figurines, posters and videos of biblical films. Other than that it was very sparse and simply furnished. I wasn't concerned about our safety, but I was glad to have Simon there. We ate at 7pm and listened to bible stories around the table. There were about six people that lived there, all men, and they each properly introduced themselves, telling us a bit about their lives and what brought them to this place. They all had a story, some were quite shocking and sad, but they convinced us that they were saved by their new-found religion. As the evening continued, we learned more about them, but we revealed very little about ourselves. Their beliefs were extreme and felt to us somewhat unhealthy.

Keeping an open mind and being respectful, we accepted their ways and appreciated their hospitality, but it was clear that we had been invited to join a cult.

Making the most of the experience we attended the weekend's events, but we were eager to leave as soon as we could. Simon slept in one caravan while Jane and I slept in the other.

One thing that I found very strange about that weekend was how they lit some lanterns on the Friday night which were to stay alight for 24 hours as on their Sabbath which is the Saturday, they say you cannot ignite flame. The lanterns went out late Saturday night and all of the residents went to bed. I had some whiskey in my hip flask and some rolling tobacco which we were desperate to smoke having abstained since we arrived. Like naughty kids we waited until all was quiet and huddled together under a tree to have our own little party. Pulling my lighter out of my pocket we went ahead to light our smokes, but it didn't work. I gave it a shake, checked the flint but there was nothing, not even a spark. It was dark and I could only assume it had run out of gas, so we abandoned the idea and went to bed. The next morning, I checked my lighter again and it worked perfectly on the first attempt. We were a bit spooked by that and all the more determined to get back to the hostel.

Trying to shake off those negative vibes we returned to Cairns. Words were left ringing in our ears of distorted beliefs about heaven and hell. We were kind of being groomed into their way of thinking but were not going to be brainwashed. Even so, it wasn't a particularly positive experience, and we felt a little disturbed. I wondered how many people over the years had been drawn in to that cult. They seemingly preyed on the desperate and the destitute which was not us. Not anymore. We were students studying at the university of life. It was good to be back.

We spent a few more weeks busking and saving money before moving on down the East coast to Townsville. Before we left, Jane and I hitched a lift up to Daintree, the rain forest and camped out amongst wild boars. It was an incredible experience. It rained continuously, we walked miles through the forest along board walks, seeing crocodiles in their natural habitat, snakes and bird eating spiders the size of my face. We pitched up a tent. There was no one else about, just us amongst nature. The forest at night was blindingly dark, except for a beam of light coming through the trees. I couldn't sleep so I took a torch and wandered cautiously towards the light trying to keep track of where I was going. The beam of light became wider. As I got closer, I stopped. Like standing at the back of an auditorium I watched as the trees, like curtains unfolding, exposed the most beautiful backdrop. The moon stood out against a huge expanse of charcoal sky. The ground beneath me became softer as I continued towards the light and I realised I was walking on sand and the waves, like symbols were crashing against the shore. There I was at night on the wildest, most primitive beach I'd ever seen with the white glow of the moon streaked across the black, enraged sea. It was breath taking.

Townsville is a coastal city in north-eastern Queensland. Only a few hours on the Greyhound from Cairns. The Strand esplanade had a pier and a rock pool which I think has now been turned into a water park. There's an aquarium which has marine life and coral from the Great Barrier Reef, plus a sea turtle hospital. Southeast of the city, the Billabong Sanctuary wildlife park is home to koalas, wombats and crocodiles. Offshore, Magnetic Island has coral reefs and a national park full of wildlife.

Townsville seemed like a good place to settle for a while, substantial in size with a great outdoor shopping mall for busking. We learned early on that we would need a permit which was encouraging as it meant that street performers were welcome. Also by having a permit we paid into the council which gave us even more of a purpose. We had to audition which was a little scary, but they loved us. It felt as though we had a proper job. We would sign in each day and set up at our designated spot.

We also joined the local folk club where we met and jammed with other musicians. The hostel was pleasant and fairly central too, so we really started to move forward with our music, getting a routine going and feeling accepted into the community. After several weeks of street performing as a duo, we met a lady called Maggie. She was a lot older than us and a very experienced singer. She too busked daily in the mall, her genre was mainly country. She had a confidence about her that was enviable. Before long we were collaborating with Maggie and working out new songs and harmonies, Maggie and I on guitars, and Jane on percussion. With the 3 vocals we had something really good going. Maggie had a strong voice and a certain presence that made her fit naturally as lead vocalist. It was plain that she had been singing and performing for years on the circuit but never really made much of it. Finding us gave her the belief that we could really go somewhere with our act. We drew in the crowds, people stopped and watched, waited around to talk to us, we were getting gig offers every day. We went from slumming it in cheap hostels to performing and staying in top notch hotels around Townsville and Magnetic Island. Soon we were contacted by the local paper to do a centre page write up about us. That was when we realised, we needed a name, so we called ourselves the 'Gypsy belles trio'. It made perfect sense. We were like gypsies, Maggie too, moving around from town to town.

If you've walked through the mall recently chances are you'd have heard the lifting harmonies of the Gypsy Belles. DEREK TIPPER reports

SISTERS IN SONG

Our biggest gig was supporting Australia's own Neil Diamond tribute act. It was a big stage in the park, with a full audience. Things were changing, we had our own unique style. I made velvet floppy hats for each of us, and our clairvoyant friend, Marg, made us matching waistcoats in midnight blue for myself, burgundy for Jane, and a rich, forest green for Maggie which complimented her big, wavy chestnut hair. We spent a lot of time together working on our music, planning our trips, travelling to gigs and socialising. What we hadn't taken into consideration though was the special dynamic that Jane and I had as a duo and had taken for granted. We were good without Maggie, people loved our sound, we had an innocence about us that people found appealing. Maggie changed that dynamic, she fronted the band with her vibrant, charismatic charm, flirting with the audience and drawing them in. We could always rely on her to put on a good show, but we started to become more like her backing singers and in time she became our boss. To begin with we felt we needed her. As she was confident and feisty, she negotiated money and secured bookings for us. Like the diva she naturally was, her attitude towards us started to become a little too pressurising and we weren't ready for that. Jane and I had a system, neither of us predominantly sang lead, we didn't argue, it just worked. For all of Maggie's professional determination and drive, she lacked team skills, she pushed us too hard, and her expectations were unrealistic. Jane and I were a strong force which I feel she resented sometimes. However, we had fun and learned a lot about ourselves and what we wanted from our music careers. The Gypsy Belles continued for the rest of our time in Townsville but what was to happen next none of us could have predicted.

It had been a few months since I'd seen Simon, he'd gone back home to the UK and although he wrote me several letters, I didn't think our relationship was strong enough to survive the long distance. We had grown apart in our pursuit of finding ourselves. Perhaps if we'd stayed together and shared experiences, we would have got close again but it wasn't to be, and I soon realised that when I became attracted to another man. His name was Shane. He was a landscape gardener for Townsville council and worked in the parks, mowing, fixing the irrigation and also tending to the flower beds in the shopping mall. Shane was well known and respected and drove around the mall in a little green cart. His uniform was standard for town council workers - navy blue shorts, polo shirt with the council logo on and brown leather work boots. He was rugged and tanned, with a great pair of legs, and the brightest, whitest toothy smile I'd ever seen. We saw him most days and one day, unexpectedly he invited us to have dinner at his house. The chance of a free meal didn't come around often so we gratefully obliged. We took our own wine and the 4 of us had a lovely evening. We ended up sleeping over. It soon became clear that there was a spark between Shane and me. As we were leaving the following day, he plucked up the courage to ask me out on a date.

Friday night Shane picked me up in his green Scirocco. He looked different, all scrubbed up, in a pair of smart jeans and an ironed shirt. His hair was combed to one side, and he was freshly shaved. I made a brief mental observation that he looked better when at work but kept that to myself. His beaming smile made up for the lack of ruggedness. He opened the passenger door for me before awkwardly pulling out a bunch of petrol station flowers. He must have watched a few films and tried to replicate the leading man but failed to be as cool. I felt a bit embarrassed but more for him than myself. We had a nice evening although a little too proper, but I realised I'd never really been treated like that before and wasn't expecting it. The following day Shane had a plan and was very excited to share it with us when he saw us in our spot in the shopping mall, setting up for the day. He was back in his scruffy work clothes, looking tanned and lovely, the Shane I was initially blown away by, and that contagious smile. His suggestion was that Jane and I move in to his spare room, rent free so we could save our money up. He didn't like that we were having to stay in a hostel dormitory with shared facilities and dirty mattresses and wanted to help us. It was an offer that we couldn't really refuse so very soon we moved in.

Nothing else changed really, we still did our own thing but before too long I had moved into Shane's room. We seemed to be establishing a relationship which felt almost too good to be true. Shane was a real gentleman, a little old fashioned in his ways and very sensible, quite unlike anyone I'd dated before. I felt different, special. I wanted to spend time with him whenever I could, but it wasn't the perfect situation. The dynamic with Jane changed, I was losing my drive and my desire to travel, Maggie wasn't keen on me dating either as it distracted me from what was important to us as a band. I was in denial and felt I could do both but the closer I became to Shane the more my ambitions started to slip. Jane could see it too. I was losing my desire to party, staying in, watching a movie appealed to me more. I didn't think it would last in all reality, falling in love was not on the agenda. There were some flaws in the relationship. He unintentionally discouraged me from busking, kindly offering money, food and accommodation so I wouldn't have to struggle anymore. He didn't understand that survival and struggling was what I was used to and actually I felt a great sense of achievement. We were working towards the bigger picture, the dream, a career in music. We had a good sound and a unique style, the world was our oyster. We had plans, we would keep travelling. We had made a list - Tasmania, New Zealand, south east Asia. Maybe not with Maggie but definitely the two of us. Staying at Shane's could work, short term if I put down some boundaries, as long as I didn't lose sight of our dream. I refused to accept too much help from Shane. I certainly couldn't fall into that trap of being reliant on him. We continued gigging, busking and partying and I told myself that soon he and I would part. I couldn't stay in Townsville indefinitely.

A friend of ours who followed our band was having a few birthday drinks one night. We all got dressed up and headed out to a lively bar in town. I wasn't feeling great, I was tired and would have preferred to stay in but knew I'd probably be fine after a few tequila's. We pulled up stools at the bar and ordered our first slammers. Hoping it would work and maybe take away the slight biliousness I was feeling, I licked the salt from my left hand and downed the tequila in one but instantly it projected from my mouth and nose. There were a few giggles from the others, but I felt the need to run to the toilet. I'd never felt like that before, I wanted to go home. I left the others to it and headed back on my own. Strangely I felt much better when I got back but went to bed early in the spare room, I needed some alone time. Shane understood and mentioned that there was a bug going around. I hoped it wasn't the beginning of Ross River fever. Maggie had told me horror stories about the virus spreading mosquito in north Queensland.

I awoke the next morning feeling even worse, there was definitely something wrong, maybe anaemia, I had gone for months on minimal food. Throughout the day I had waves of sickness and extreme tiredness, I couldn't go out busking, it was so hot out. I sipped water and Shane made me soup when he returned from work, I managed to keep it down but started to be very concerned. Jane wanted to go out, we went out a lot previously, drinking, dancing and jamming with musicians. I couldn't do it. A few days later when I was still bad, I thought about going to the doctor's, something was definitely wrong, I was scared. I remember sitting on the steps of Shane's house with Jane. she asked me when I had my last period. I don't know why I found that such a ridiculous question, but she wasn't to know that Shane and I were very careful. I had never really kept tabs on when I was due. I just kind of knew and I was sure I wasn't late. Jane and I were usually in sync, and she worked out quickly that I had missed a period. I knew I couldn't have been pregnant, we did everything to prevent it but just to be sure I bought a test.

Jane and Shane waited outside the bathroom; I felt silly, I had a bug that was all. A few minutes later I was staring at the test strip, it had 2 blue lines. There must have been a mistake. When I showed the others, they looked as confused and shocked as I did. Shane immediately booked me an appointment with his doctor, I got booked in the next day. Still very sick I went along hoping we'd get to the bottom of what it was I had. The doctor felt my stomach and pelvis and proceeded with an internal inspection and said that I definitely wasn't pregnant. He confirmed that those tests were unreliable and that particular one was most probably faulty. With a sense of relief I left, but still no more informed as to why I felt so ill and was very frustrated. A couple of weeks passed and there was no improvement, Maggie insisted I took a blood test to rule out Ross River fever as I was losing weight and money and was desperately anxious and worried. I considered going back to England, the heat was becoming too much to bear. I was getting cramps from lack of salt. I thought about my mother's illness and whether I might have cancer, all I wanted to do was sleep. A few days later I checked in to see another doctor, a lady this time. I told her my symptoms and she took a urine test. Within a few moments she smiled at me and said, "Anna you are pregnant." I struggled to make sense of her words, I had no idea how I was supposed to feel and what to do with that information, all I knew was that I wasn't dying, and the relief was enormous. I wasn't ill but I was growing a child inside me, how could that be and what was I going to do? Shane was great, he wanted to support me, he seemed excited and wanted to be a dad. Maggie suggested I have a termination, Jane said she would support any decision I made. As far as I was concerned, I was going to be a mother whether convenient or not. I loved this child already.

We did a few gigs, but they were thinning out, most of our work came from busking in the mall and I was struggling to keep it going. Plans had to be put on hold. Jane wanted to go back to Sydney.

Maggie was really disappointed in me. I had no idea what to do but the heat was making me feel sicker. I did not understand why it was called morning sickness, I felt nauseous all the time.

I was alone in Australia with just Shane now and my life had completely changed direction. My body was changing shape too. I hardly touched my guitar, just sat around Shane's house whilst he was at work, listening to Celine Dion, drinking ginger tea and nurturing my growing bump.

I wasn't very happy living there, but I was calm and a little complacent. One day I called Vicky in England, and she suggested I come home, I hadn't really thought of it as a possibility, but the idea really appealed to me. The seed had been planted in more ways than one! I couldn't stop thinking about England. I knew I had to go.

Unfortunately, I soon realised I didn't love Shane, the honeymoon period had worn off a bit. I certainly hoped that I could and maybe would in time. He tried to do everything right but the one thing that played on my mind was that he didn't get my desire and passion for music. I think he saw it as something

I would grow out of. My suggestion that he followed me back to England went down like a lead balloon. It was possible for him to get holiday leave, he could definitely afford to, but he wouldn't consider it. How could he ever really know me if he hadn't seen my country and met my friends and family? It was the one compromise that he could have made which might have changed everything. I wasn't suggesting him leaving his whole life behind and never returning but maybe an extended visit. I hadn't ruled out living in Australia but just needed to be home for a while. I'd been living in a dream world. My life had again been turned upside down. I couldn't plan my future until I'd faced my past, spoken to my friends and family. Looked at my options and seen the reality of everything from my side of the world.

Chapter 7

'Lost for words'

I'm lost for words, no words can say how I adore you,
I'm lost in love, no other love can feel like our love.

My thoughts are going round and round, I can't hear a
single sound, except for all the words in my mind, when
I try to say to you the words that I am longing to, those
simple words are so hard to find.

I'm lost for words what can I say?

I'm lost for words and every day I'm lost for words, do
you feel what I feel?

I'm lost for words, do you feel the same way?

Reality hit me in many ways. I returned to a cold frosty winter. Knocking on the door of my brother Patrick's house with my problems was becoming quite a habit but this time I had another human growing inside me. I was grateful for the warm-hearted welcome they gave me. I moved in with them, properly this time. Patrick even converted the loft for me. Without needing to explain anything or justify my messy life, they took me in and gave me the love and emotional security that I had been wanting for years. I had changed, with the growing baby inside me and I put all my ambitions of being a professional musician aside. There may be time in the future but for now I was to be the best mother that I could be.

I found a job working in a hot potato van, quite appropriate as my bump continued to get bigger. I was an advert for potatoes. I loved the job, my boss was great, a big body builder, also an advert for potatoes. We sold lots; all of Henley's celebrities from George Harrison to Nigel Havers lunched at our van, grabbing a snack on their way to or from Waitrose.

I also had the honourable job of child minding my niece and nephew, so I kept myself busy up until a week before I was due to give birth.

Oliver Benjamin Watts came into the world on the 19th of April 1994.

My best friend, Vicky, was my birthing partner. It was the first most incredible experience I had ever had. I looked at that perfect little person as they lay him on my belly, still attached to the umbilical cord and wondered how it was possible to feel so happy. I was lost for words.

There are only a few times in my life when I have been lost for words. The expression itself is a good one as the greatest writers in the world can probably confirm that they too have felt the same.

When a feeling is so deep, no word can do it justice. When love is unconditional somehow the word 'love' is not enough. My song 'Lost for words' is very simple lyrically, the sentiment is formed by the tune and the overlapping of verses. We wanted it to sound like angels flying around singing in the biggest cathedral imaginable. The track was recorded with my singing partner at the time, Jane Kelly, whom I began Hennesea with. We layered up vocals with lots of reverb in the harmonies and had my guitar sounding like a harp. I was overwhelmed by the finished result. It's like two songs in one. I wrote the two lots of lyrics in a way that they fit when sung together. I love the track, the recording was engineered at the Old Smithy Studio. It's very difficult to replicate it live with the same magical feel about it, especially as Jane is no longer in the band. Something to work on in the future with our other vocalist.

Oliver is now 29. He shared quite an adventure with me. We stayed in Henley for about 5 months and then we moved to France close to where my dad lived. I had a one -bedroom flat above a bar. It was clean and warm, but I struggled to support us both. Apart from my brother, Daniel, 14 already, visiting on occasions I was very lonely. I couldn't speak French and it was very difficult to make friends, so we moved back to Henley again for a short while. An old friend of my mother's had a spare room in his Henley town house. He was a bookbinder and a fabulous musician. He never married or had children and he had no patience at all with Oliver who was at the age of pulling himself around the furniture and putting everything in his mouth. On the day I caught him rubbing my son's face in spilt milk was the day I decided to leave.

I called Shane in Australia. I had run out of options, and it was time for father and son to meet. I had hoped he would visit us but that wasn't to be so instead he paid for our tickets to go and visit him.

Oliver was 9 months old and had just taken his first steps. There was no stopping him now. He had a big cheeky smile like his father and blond curls, he was my pride and joy.

The plane journey was exhausting, he toddled up and down the aisle, tumbling over and getting back up, grinning at everybody. We arrived in Townsville during the hottest time of the year. It was almost unbearable. There was a cyclone heading towards us, everyone was taping up their windows and tying down their garden furniture. It was building up strength over the sea and already a category 4. I was naturally worried for our safety, but Shane convinced me that it was a good thing as it would bring in a lot of much needed rain especially to farmland and it's unlikely that the eye would hit Townsville. Although encouraged by his positive outlook I still expected the worst, I had visions of Shane's house lifting off the ground and spinning through the sky with all of us in it. I couldn't sleep, the humidity was like nothing I'd ever experienced before. I drenched my bed sheets under the shower, folded them up and put them in the freezer, this became a daily thing. Unwrapping the crisp icy square and wrapping it around my body was heaven.

Well, it's fair to say that Shane fell in love with Oliver the moment he set eyes on him. He looked the image of his father with his white toothy smile. It was a relief to share that love and responsibility.

Life became a lot easier. When Ollie was ill, we shared the concern, when he needed new clothes Shane would buy them. What we had previously as a couple been lost in a whirl of time and troubles, surviving as a single mother. We tried to reignite that spark. I wanted to love him. It would have been the perfect happy ending, but I just didn't feel it. It felt enough that he loved our son and I respected and valued Shane as a good friend.

My visa was for 6 months only, and I was worried about returning to England with nowhere to live again. Ollie was my priority now so when Shane proposed marriage to me, I accepted. It meant I would be able to stay and apply for residency. It was a decision we came to very casually at the Australian immigration office and so I felt we were both on the same page.

We kept things simple and got married in the Botanical Gardens. It was an understated, modest wedding, very casual with a few of Shane's closest friends and family. We finished the day off with a barbeque in Shane's back yard.

Oliver and I in the kangaroo sanctuary.

Over time it became clear that Shane wanted and expected more of me as his wife and he tried so hard to make me happy. He was a good husband and a lovely father. However, by trying too hard it just made things worse between us. He told me I was incapable of loving any man and I wondered if maybe he was right. I started to detach from myself as I considered that I was my own enemy. My life had become a sequence of bad decisions, the only right and good thing in my life was the child that I'd brought into the world, and I had to protect that good thing and trust the people in my life that were helping me. My wants and needs were no longer important.

I started to suffer terribly with eczema from head to toe. I was wearing bandages around my bleeding arms at night and the rest of my body looked like it was covered in cling film. I became tired all the time from lack of sleep, and I couldn't cope with the endless stifling heat. I put my heart and soul into trying to make things work with Shane but patient as he was with me, waiting for me to fall in love with him, it didn't happen. I soon realised it never would. I also realised that he never really knew the whole me, just a version of me.

An old friend I'd met with Jane found out that I was back in Townsville. She was a real gypsy, her name was Marg, she made our Gypsy Belles waist coats. An interesting character that read palms. One day when Shane was at work there was a knock at the door. I didn't have visitors often, I had become very much a loner. Wearing just a sarong exposing my red, cracked, itchy skin I answered the door. It was her. With her colourful clothes, gold jewellery and bright pink lipstick, she was a sight for sore eyes. I threw my arms around her. The familiar smell of white musk filled my nostrils. This was a lady that somehow knew me well without having known me long.

She stood back, took one look at me and said, "Darling, you must go home." My first response was defensive, I was doing my best, I was making it work. Marg took my hand and stroked my palm before holding it up towards her inquisitive eyes, reading me as simply as if I was a book. She told me again, "You must go home." I didn't understand, Ollie was the important one, my happiness was irrelevant. I made Marg a cup of chamomile tea and we chatted. I didn't want to hear what she was saying, it was too much, too hard to consider anything other than this life I had now chosen. After she left, I was completely confused, almost cross with her. Her words stuck in my head, I tried to forget and ignore her advice but there it was, and I was questioning myself again.

Ollie was 2 years old when we returned to England, a lot had changed, I had nowhere to live, I was back to where I was before, homeless. It was the middle of winter, thick snow on the ground. My only option was the little log cabin which had been sat derelict. There was a bed in there with musty damp blankets. There was portable gas heater which worked and warmed the place up nicely but it woke up the hibernating wasp nest and I spent the whole night shooing them away so Ollie could sleep. The next day I had to reassess my situation.

My Australian travel partner, Jane, was living in Malvern, at the time. She had enjoyed England so much so had returned to stay with her cousins for a while - James and Steve who had both moved there into a large shared house. It seemed like the perfect opportunity to go and visit them. I borrowed some money off Patrick and bought a cheap car. He and Les were helpful and understanding and said I could stay with them, but my grandmother interfered and told me to find my own place. She was furious that I'd come back and was potentially going to be a burden on them all. I took Gran's advice. With tears running down my cheeks I drove the 2-hour journey up through the Cotswolds with Ollie strapped into the passenger seat. The drive was actually beautiful, everything was dusted with snow. I had been given rough directions through all the little towns and villages. I had the radio playing; we sang, we laughed, and I cried, all the while Ollie beside me with his big blue eyes and cheeky smile.

I had no idea what to expect once I got to Malvern, but it turned out to be the best decision I ever made. We pulled up outside a very large house made from Malvern stone. I thought we were at the wrong place until I saw Steve waving from the middle floor window which was the kitchen. He looked as excited to see me and Ollie as I was to see his familiar, friendly face. We walked into the big lobby where there were doors leading to the landlord's living quarters and up to the second floor to where the lodgers lived. It was rather run down, and I couldn't help but notice the worn fraying carpet on the stair treads. It all felt very homely and welcoming though. Jane had got a temping job and was still at work, but Steve was in between lorry driving jobs and had just come back from the shops with a cake mix. When I called to say I was coming he got treats in for Ollie. I was touched by that gesture. After the three of us finished baking the little cupcakes, we left them to cool off and Steve took us swimming at the local pool just 5 minutes' walk down the road. Later Jane came home. We had so much to catch up on and she hadn't yet met my little boy.

James was working at a garage in Malvern and soon returned home. He was shocked and pleasantly surprised to see us. I was even more surprised to see how he had grown into himself. As a teenager he was a slow developer, his wiry legs were accentuated by his skin-tight jeans and the mop of bushy brown hair fell over his eyes that were a just a little too widely set. When he appeared in front of me with his shortly cropped, jelled back hair and well-proportioned physique I couldn't help but notice what a fine-looking man he had become.

We all cooked dinner, opened a bottle of wine and talked till dawn. It was wonderful being around people that really knew me. When they all persuaded me to stay, I called Patrick and told him the news. He was annoyed with gran for making me leave but in hind sight it was probably the best thing she ever did for me.

The bedrooms were huge, with bay windows and fire places. James had two beds in his room and after running it by Andy, the house owner, it was agreed that I could stay there for as long as it took to get myself sorted. Everything just fell into place.

In Paradise

*There are times when I like to dance, times when I like
to sing, sometimes I just sit around not do anything.*

*When I'm alone I can think, when I'm with friends I can
laugh, in paradise I feel I can do all of these things.*

*There's a place I go where the sun is always shining,
faces in the clouds smile, trees like dancers in the
breeze reach out to me and I know I'm never alone in
paradise.*

*Sometimes I feel I could cry, at times I could just curl
up and die but when I am weak, I know I can speak out
my paradise*

*I can sing with the birds in the trees, dance around in
the falling leaves, laugh with the ghosts of the past, I
can do all of these things*

*In the place I go where the sun is always shining, faces
in the clouds smile, trees like dancers in the breeze
reach out to me and I know I'm never alone in paradise.*

I didn't return to Henley. Malvern accepted me, I felt proud
of my status. I applied for single parent benefit for a short
time until I'd got myself settled and found work. I got my own
place, a one-bedroom cottage and James moved in with me. Our
relationship started one night after a few drinks. I didn't see it
coming, he was my brother's best friend, we'd been on family
holidays together, he drove me to work when I was 17. I never
saw him in a romantic light and yet we became best friends and
life partners.

Chapter 8

3 0 years later and I'm still here in Malvern. Married to my childhood friend, James. He loved Ollie like his own and we had 2 more sons together, Charlie and Adam. We bought a beautiful big house, filled it with love, fun and chaos. Of all the places in the world I could have ended up I feel my roller coaster life led me to the greatest place on earth that I could be. It was quite a journey and took many lessons to arrive here but looking back on past events and piecing them together I now realise that everything in my life happened for a reason. I had found my home, my music and my paradise.

Shane and I kept in touch, but he still hasn't been to England. I'm hoping that Ollie will seek him out one day. Ollie left home at 18 to live in Bristol. He is a carpenter and travels around the country in his camper van putting together big festivals like Glastonbury and Boomtown. Charlie and Adam live here in Malvern. My foster sons, Pav, Dan, Lewis and Jo, also grown up now are doing really well and are a big part of my life too.

Mandolin man

His face tells a story of a million rainy days, his eyes show a deepness in a thousand different ways.

His hair is thin, his body is worn, his clothes are ragged, and they're torn but he lights up the darkness with the music that he plays

As the leaves fall to the ground Mandolin man is heading south to bluer skies and warmer nights, sleeping under the moonlight

Bag on back and mandolin, everybody smiles at him because he lights up the darkness with the music that he plays

They call him Mandolin man 'cause no one knows his name, no one knows his story, no one knows his pain, but I wish he'd play to me tonight sitting by the fire light, his songs lift the darkness until morning is in sight

Farewell Mandolin man, I wish I knew your name, I wish that I had met you before you went away

But you have left a memory that I'll take to my grave with me, it's a song you were playing when you brightened up my day.

Mandolin man is on our first album, 'Lost for words.' I wrote it in the early days of forming the band here in Malvern. We still perform it live and it's become a favourite of ours. Another Malvern band cover, 'The Dublin Jacks' fronted by my good friend Ray Hadden. He has helped me out a lot in the past years. He made me a leather pouch belt which holds all of my harmonicas. He also made me a leather guitar strap with my name on. He designed it based on how I described my mum's old strap from South America with the red roses down the middle.

Ray has a theory about the meaning behind my song 'Mandolin man.' As I've previously pointed out that songs can be entirely fictional as is 'Mandolin man' I often tell a story on stage about it being someone I met on my travels. When you are performing to an audience, you are basically acting so it's completely ok to dramatize. People like it. Whether it's true or not, it helps to paint that picture for them and awaken the imagination. Ray's theory, however, is that I am the Mandolin man in the story. I can see his point and I'm actually quite flattered that he would think that. Maybe he's right in some ways but with song writing, there is no right or wrong. There are good songs and there are bad songs.

Last year for my birthday the boys bought me a ticket to Nashville so I could fulfil my childhood dream. I travelled alone which brought back a lot of nostalgic feelings. I loved the sense of freedom and adventure, most of all was the unknown. I'd be lying if I said I wasn't nervous, flying terrifies me. It had been years since I'd been away without James and the boys, and I certainly had mixed feelings about it.

At 4 am James dropped me off at Heathrow airport with a small case. I didn't take my guitar, I figured I would buy a second hand one out there. After checking in I sat in the bar and had a pint of beer for breakfast. My holiday had begun. I had the best travel buddy, a lovely lady from Boston; we chatted the whole way and exchanged contact details. As soon as I arrived in Nashville, I headed for the taxi depot and got a cab to take me straight to my Airbnb. This was my first time in America. I had gone to Canada with my parents in my teens, but this was a whole new experience. When I arrived at the house there was a note on the door with instructions of how to get into my apartment, the hosts were out at the time. There wasn't a soul in site. It was a nice quiet area. I let myself in and made myself at home. The hosts appeared a couple of hours later, Jason and Megan, and I introduced myself. They were both musicians and they very kindly lent me a guitar for the duration of my stay. They informed me of all the events going on and places to check out. Feeling exhausted I decided to get an early night so unpacked, had some peanuts for my supper washed down with a bottle of Bud Light.

Lying there on my bed I started to feel a bit strange. An overwhelming wave of fear came over me for no apparent reason. The sun hadn't quite gone down, and it was light in my room, so I just lay there, unable to sleep and too tired to read. That was when the panic started. My heart was racing, my chest felt tight, and I was terrified that I would die, and no one would know about it. Calming myself with deep breaths I managed to slow my heart rate down and tried to meditate until I eventually dozed off for a few hours.

The next day, I called an Uber and went downtown. From the moment I got out of the cab and for the rest of my time in Nashville I literally couldn't take the smile off my face. Downtown Nashville was vibrant. From 11 am the bands started playing in every bar along the boulevard, music from every window on every level of the tall buildings, even on the roofs. The quality of music was sublime. There was rock and country, old and modern. Musicians of all ages, bands, soloists, duos. I was spoilt for choice. I got the hang of the tipping rule when buying a beer and there were ATMs in every bar to tip the musicians cash. They relied on it and they worked so hard, barely taking a break for 4 to 8 hours, selling their souls singing covers to the tourists, pleasing the punters with their polished renditions of popular songs.

There was an underlying sadness that I couldn't help but feel. Every musician there had star quality and I'm sure would love to be discovered but the boulevard wasn't the place to play their own songs. Sitting there at the bar with a bottle of Bud, people watching, I learned that the majority of folk wanted to hear their own voices, whilst catching glimpses of themselves in the mirror dancing in their Daisy Duke shorts and cowboy boots.

I was drawn to a girl in her 20's. She was patiently and very professionally meeting the demands of a group of bachelorettes on their weekend out. She could play just about everything she was asked. She was like a human jukebox. Very good, I couldn't fault her, but I couldn't see, feel or hear her soul in her voice, like a machine spinning the sounds out whilst the drunken girls drowned her out with their high-pitched wailing, laughter and singing out of key.

She held it together like a true professional, but I could see the frustration in her eyes and boredom. It was just another day at work for her. Before another cheesy song was shouted out by a demanding punter, I pulled a 20 dollar bill out of the ATM and handed it to the singer with my request; an original. She looked at me questioningly, so I said just to be safe, "Your favourite song, cover or original but original if you have one." This was the moment that the girl became real, a little uncomfortable at first whilst she announced her song and the story behind it, but she had a sparkle in her eyes, a little sadness too as she tuned into the deepest part of herself. Her discomfort was there but she masked it well and like a troubadour she told her story through the breath-taking tones of her voice and the subtle picking of her guitar strings. The room went quiet allowing her space to project at the level and tempo that was needed. She was in her element for that short time, a little nervous but human and real as she exposed her soul and I felt privileged to be there.

There was so much to do and too little time to do everything. I was thankful to the fact that I chose to stay in the suburbs of east Nashville. It was for me the most un-tourist decision I made. I wanted to meet the residents, find the local bars and hang out with Nashville folk so that's exactly what I did.

On the list of places to go, my host, Jason put down 'Fran's Eastside Diner.' It's a karaoke bar which isn't my thing at all, but I thought I'd check it out. The Uber pulled up outside a particularly unappealing glass fronted building. I spotted a few pool tables and fruit machines and was a little hesitant to go in, but the Uber had left, and it was too far to walk anywhere else. At the back of the building was a bar that stretched the whole width of the smoke-filled room with a row of backs sat at stools. As I entered, a whole line of heads turned and stared at me. Mostly bearded, tattooed truck driver types with baseball caps and cowboy hats and a man that looked like Nat King Cole. The bartender with her long white hair that hung down to below her Daisy Duke shorts must have been in her 70's. She looked at me questioningly as I asked for a beer. "We only serve beer," she said, to which point I ordered a Bud Light and sat on the only available bar stool. The line of men on either side of me continued to stare so I took my phone out my bag and feeling a little intimidated tried to busy myself. A man that sat right at the end of the bar looked like a member of the band ZZ Top. He called the bartender over and had a word in her ear. She then came to me with another bottle of Bud, "Courtesy of Huck," she said, "and he wants you to put your phone away and start being more sociable," so I did as I was told and as the evening went on I bought them all a round of beers, joined in with the karaoke, danced with the Nat King Cole look alike who was an absolute gentleman, "I'm Nipples" he said, I didn't ask! I had a really great night. My clothes and hair reeked of smoke, so I showered before going to bed that night and put a wash on. I think that was renowned to be one of the roughest dives that still exists in Nashville but the people there were absolute diamonds. They made sure I got in my cab and waved me off.

The highlight of my trip was singing two of my own songs on a stage at an open mic. The experience was incredible. I was advised by my hosts at the bnb to turn up at 5pm as people come from all over to perform their songs and you have to get your name down on the list. My hosts very kindly lent me a guitar. It was my second day in Nashville, I was like a fish out of water. The bar was fairly small and intimate with a sitting down audience, the stage was cosy with pretty lamps and cowboy boots neatly placed all around the edge, there was a red velvet curtained backdrop, and the stage floor was black. Behind the stage was where the musicians would go and tune up 10 minutes before their turn. I looked around the room at all the cool-headed musicians. They'd done this before and seemed to all know each other. I was alone and nervous, looking for a friendly face to console me. I found one, his name was Butch. I knew just by my first impression that he was going to be amazingly good and then I met Holly. She was lovely, she smiled and cheered every act that played. Jennifer hosted the open mic, and she too was friendly and made me feel welcome. I was still scared, I imagined I would be boo'd off the stage. How could my songs stand up here, the music city of the world? I felt silly, how could I possibly compete? 3 names were called out to prepare to play. I'd had one bottle of Bud Light, just enough to ease my nerves. My name came through the microphone as Anna from London. I moved backstage with my guitar and waited for the 2 girls in front of me to finish. They were good, young and confident. Finally, I was called on to the stage, I put my harmonica holder on and placed the C harp into it whilst the audience sat quietly watching. I checked the levels on my guitar and then introduced myself. The audience was quiet but smiling. My harp intro broke the silence and sounded good, just the right amount of reverb coming through the monitors and then I sang the words 'His face tells a story of a million rainy days'. The fold back was perfect and through it my voice felt and sounded good, controlled and clear. I relaxed into it, cast my eyes around the room and smiled. I pulled it off, the audience clapped and kept smiling as I played my next song. Afterwards I sat myself down, ordered a large bourbon and enjoyed the rest of the evening feeling incredible. I had sung on a stage in Nashville! Now I was no longer a stranger, people spoke to me, accepted me. I was one of them, floating on the same boat of songwriters but on the other side of the pond.

My first open mic in Nashville.

My favourite bar in the whole of Nashville was Dee's Cocktail Lounge in Madison. It was very basically three or four trailers stitched together, with a wooden veranda at the front. There was a nicely lit stage at the back with live bands playing every night. That place became my local and it's where I made some lovely friends who welcomed me and made the effort to get to know me a bit. For them I was just someone passing through but for me, those faces I will never forget.

People wonder why I still get nervous playing live, after all these years. I am naturally shy. I hate that I am shy and every day at some point I find myself feeling embarrassed, blushing or getting into an uncomfortable state about something. I ask myself the question every time I put myself out there to perform, why? ...Because it makes me feel alive and because I have something I want to share. When I first get up in front of a room of people, however many there may be, I can only see as far as my microphone. Similar to when you first drive a car, you can only see to the end of the bonnet and the road immediately in front whilst trying to keep the car in a straight line. Alternatively, you're out running, your legs feel heavy, your heart is racing and you don't know what to do with your arms. My nerves keep me restricted in my own little bubble, I'm out of breath from my racing heart and my mouth is dry. Then I warm into it and the flood of adrenaline subsides, the bubble disperses and the room opens up. That is when I can look out at the people all around me, when I can connect with the audience, my heart slows down and I just want to keep on going and giving it my very best.

I'm 53 years old now. We've recorded four albums 'Lost for words' 'Shine on' 'Book of life' and 'Laced with gold'. I plan to keep on writing, performing and learning. My newest song I hope to have recorded by the time I finish this book. It's called 'Danser dans la nuit' (Dance in the night). It fits well with 'Faisons comme si' (Let's pretend) which is on the album 'Laced with gold.'

I hope I haven't offended anyone or missed out anything important; if so, it wasn't intentional. This has been a well-needed cathartic exercise. Writing this book has reconnected me to times and events that I rarely thought or spoke about. It has pieced things together in my mind, sorted out the good and bad stuff. Filed things away in the proper order and encouraged me to look at myself in a new light.

The events in our lives certainly mould us, every incident, every failing, tragic occurrences and the people we meet all have an impact on our lives. Everything we learn is in preparation for our future. Everything we experience we can pass on, teach, advise and warn others of but fundamentally each one of us is unique and the things we don't like about ourselves, if we cannot change, we must learn to accept. Education and training can fill you with knowledge, but life will teach you wisdom and how to survive. If you have a voice, use it, nobody can tell your story like you can. If you write a song, sing it, nobody can share the emotion like you can. If you have words to share.... write.

Jane has been living back home in Australia for the last 30 years with her husband and children but she came to visit me in England and sang a few songs with my band and me. It was magical and so great to be finally reunited after all these years.

Book of life

Memories are like pages in my book of life,

I turn back a chapter to a different time,

looking for the words that lay between the lines,

I turn back the pages, contemplate the stages of my book of life.

In the corner of the room there is an empty chair and a window looking out into the night, a candle by the bedside a clock against the wall, a picture of a face in black and white.

Stories unfold all the memories in me,

my life's a story and I hold the key,

to unlock the secrets, those secrets in me, I hold the book and the book holds the key.

I see the story changing now before my eyes

Making life a mystery and mystery is nice

Until I reach the end, I will not see what lies ahead So,

I turn back the pages, contemplate the stages of my book of life.

Stories unfold all the memories in me

My life's a story and I hold the key

To unlock the secrets, those secrets in me

I hold the book and the book holds the key.

Hennesea are a five-piece new folk-rock band from Malvern in Worcestershire. They regularly play gigs and festivals around the UK and the music is available on Spotify,

Amazon and on CD from their website. Anna Lindahl, the singer and guitar player with the band has Scandinavian roots. The word Hennesea comes from the Swedish 'hennes' which means 'hers'. The band's first full album came out in 2015. 'Book of Life' features a baker's dozen of eclectic ensemble pieces that range from the winsome title track to the magnificent 'Light Above the Sea'. The latter features Martin Furey of The High Kings on backing vocals and flute. Mark Keene plays guitar and mandolin while Garry Low is on drums and percussion. Garry is also an accomplished recording engineer and has been responsible for engineering and producing Hennesea's releases. In 2016, Ralph Tittley joined Hennesea on bass guitar and backing vocals. Since then, the band has played many gigs and festivals, including the BBC Stage at Lake Fest, Mappfest, Sunshine Festival, Mello and Cwm Fest. They have played at every Malvern Rocks since it began. The latest album, 'Laced with Gold', was released in January 2021 and includes the singles 'The Same Tune' and 'Faison Comme Si'. Since 2019, Hennesea have been joined on stage by Rob Murray-Mason. He began sound mixing the gigs, but soon was adding percussion and backing vocals and is now integral to the sound of the band. Hennesea always puts on a good show and never disappoints.

Milton Keynes UK
Ingram Content Group UK Ltd.
UKHW020937231123
433129UK00016B/700